2020-2021

CPC PRACTICE EXAMINATION (2020-2021)

Full Answer Key & Rationale

THE CODERS CHOICE, LLC

1. 46 year-old female had a previous biopsy that indicated positive malignant margins anteriorly on the right side of her neck. A 0.5 cm margin was drawn out and a 15 blade scalpel was used for full excision of an 8 cm lesion. Layered closure was performed after the removal. The specimen was sent for permanent histopathologic examination. What are the CPT® code(s) for this procedure?

A. 11626

B. 11626, 12004-51

C. 11626, 12044-51

D. 11626, 13132-51, 13133

2. 30 year-old female is having 15 sq. cm debridement performed on an infected ulcer with eschar on the right foot. Using sharp dissection, the ulcer was debrided all the way to down to the bone of the foot. The bone had to be minimally trimmed because of a sharp point at the end of the metatarsal. After debriding the area, there was minimal bleeding because of very poor circulation of the foot. It seems that the toes next to the ulcer may have some involvement and cultures were taken. The area was dressed with sterile saline and dressings and then wrapped. What CPT® code should be reported?

A. 11043

B. 11012

C. 11044

D. 11042

3. 64 year-old female who has multiple sclerosis fell from her walker and landed on a glass table. She lacerated her forehead, cheek and chin and the total length of these lacerations was 6 cm. Her right arm and left leg had deep cuts measuring 5 cm on each extremity. Her right hand and right foot had a total of 3 cm lacerations. The ED physician repaired the lacerations as follows: The forehead, cheek, and chin had debridement and cleaning of glass debris with the lacerations being closed with one layer closure, 6-0 Prolene sutures. The arm and leg were repaired by layered closure, 6-0 Vicryl subcutaneous sutures and Prolene sutures on the skin. The hand and foot were closed with adhesive strips. Select the appropriate procedure codes for this visit.

A. 99283-25, 12014, 12034-59, 12002-59, 11042-51

B. 99283-25, 12053, 12034-59, 12002-59

C. 99283-25, 12014, 12034-59, 11042-51

D. 99283-25, 12053, 12034-59

4. 52 year-old female has a mass growing on her right flank for several years. It has finally gotten significantly larger and is beginning to bother her. She is brought to the Operating Room for definitive excision. An incision was made directly overlying the mass. The mass was down into the subcutaneous tissue and the surgeon encountered a well encapsulated lipoma approximately 4 centimeters. This was excised primarily bluntly with a few attachments divided with electrocautery. What CPT® and ICD-10-CM codes are reported?

A. 21932, D17.39

B. 21935, D17.1

C. 21931, D17.1

D. 21925, D17.9

5. PREOPERATIVE DIAGNOSIS: Right scaphoid fracture.

   TYPE OF PROCEDURE: Open reduction and internal fixation of right scaphoid fracture.

   DESCRIPTION OF PROCEDURE: The patient was brought to the operating room; anesthesia having been administered. The right upper extremity was prepped and draped in a sterile manner. The limb was elevated, exsanguinated, and a pneumatic arm tourniquet was elevated. An incision was made over the dorsal radial aspect of the right wrist. Skin flaps were elevated. Cutaneous nerve branches were identified and very gently retracted. The interval between the second and third dorsal compartment tendons was identified and entered. The respective tendons were retracted. A dorsal capsulotomy incision was made, and the fracture was visualized. There did not appear to be any type of significant defect at the fracture site. A 0.045 Kirschner wire was then used as a guidewire, extending from the proximal pole of the scaphoid distal ward. The guidewire was positioned appropriately and then measured. A 25-mm Acutrak® drill bit was drilled to 25 mm. A 22.5-mm screw was selected and inserted and rigid internal fixation was accomplished in this fashion. This was visualized under the OEC imaging device in multiple projections. The wound was irrigated and closed in layers. Sterile dressings were then applied. The patient tolerated the procedure well and left the operating room in stable condition. What CPT® code is reported for this procedure?

A. 25628-RT

B. 25624-RT

C. 25645-RT

D. 25651-RT

6. An infant with genu valgum is brought to the operating room to have a bilateral medial distal femur hemiepiphysiodesis done. On each knee, the C-arm was used to localize the growth plate. With the growth plate localized, an incision was made medially on both sides. This was taken down to the fascia, which was opened. The periosteum was not opened. The Orthofix® figure-of-eight plate was placed and checked with X-ray. We then irrigated and closed the medial fascia with 0 Vicryl suture. The skin was closed with 2-0 Vicryl and 3-0 Monocryl®. What procedure code is reported?

A. 27470-50

B. 27475-50

C. 27477-50

D. 27485-50

7. The patient is a 67 year-old gentleman with metastatic colon cancer recently operated on for a brain metastasis, now for placement of an Infuse-A-Port for continued chemotherapy. The left subclavian vein was located with a needle and a guide wire placed. This was confirmed to be in the proper position fluoroscopically. A transverse incision was made just inferior to this and a subcutaneous pocket created just inferior to this. After tunneling, the introducer was placed over the guide wire and the power port line was placed with the introducer and the introducer was peeled away. The tip was placed in the appropriate position under fluoroscopic guidance and the catheter trimmed to the appropriate length and secured to the power port device. The locking mechanism was fully engaged. The port was placed in the subcutaneous pocket and everything sat very nicely fluoroscopically. It was secured to the underlying soft tissue with 2-0 silk stitch. What CPT® code(s) is (are) reported for this procedure?

A. 36556, 77001-26

B. 36558

C. 36561, 77001-26

D. 36571

8. A CT scan identified moderate-sized right pleural effusion in a 50 year-old male. This was estimated to be 800 cc in size and had an appearance of fluid on the CT scan. A needle is used to puncture through the chest tissues and enter the pleural cavity to insert a guidewire under ultrasound guidance. A pigtail catheter is then inserted at the length of the guidewire and secured by stitches. The catheter will remain in the chest and is connected to drainage system to drain the accumulated fluid. The CPT® code is:

A. 32557

B. 32555

C. 32556

D. 32550

9. The patient is a 59 year-old white male who underwent carotid endarterectomy for symptomatic left carotid stenosis a year ago. A carotid CT angiogram showed a recurrent 90% left internal carotid artery stenosis extending into the common carotid artery. He is taken to the operating room for re-do left carotid endarterectomy. The left neck was prepped and the previous incision was carefully reopened. Using sharp dissection, the common carotid artery and its branches were dissected free. The patient was systematically heparinized and after a few minutes, clamps were applied to the common carotid artery and its branches. A longitudinal arteriotomy was carried out with findings of extensive layering of intimal hyperplasia with no evidence of recurrent atherosclerosis. A silastic balloon-tip shunt was inserted first proximally and then distally, with restoration of flow. Several layers of intima were removed and the endarterectomized surfaces irrigated with heparinized saline. An oval Dacron patch was then sewn into place with running 6-0 Prolene. Which CPT® code(s) is/are reported?

A. 35301

B. 35301, 35390

C. 35302

D. 35311, 35390

10. A 52 year-old patient is admitted to the hospital for chronic cholecystitis for which a laparoscopic cholecystectomy will be performed. A transverse infraumbilical incision was made sharply dissecting to the subcutaneous tissue down to the fascia using access under direct vision with a Vesi-Port and a scope was placed into the abdomen. Three other ports were inserted under direct vision. The fundus of the gallbladder was grasped through the lateral port, where multiple adhesions to the gallbladder were taken down sharply and bluntly: The gallbladder appeared chronically inflamed. Dissection was carried out to the right of this identifying a small cystic duct and artery, was clipped twice proximally, once distally and transected. The gallbladder was then taken down from the bed using electrocautery, delivering it into an endo-bag and removing it from the abdominal cavity with the umbilical port. What CPT® and ICD-10-CM codes are reported?

A. 47564, K81.2

B. 47562, K81.1

C. 47610, K81.2

D. 47600, K81.1

11. A 70 year-old female who has a history of symptomatic ventral hernia was advised to undergo laparoscopic evaluation and repair. An incision was made in the epigastrium and dissection was carried down through the subcutaneous tissue. Two 5-mm trocars were placed, one in the left upper quadrant and one in the left lower quadrant and the laparoscope was inserted. Dissection was carried down to the area of the hernia where a small defect was clearly visualized. There was some omentum, which was adhered to the hernia and this was delivered back into the peritoneal cavity. The mesh was tacked on to cover the defect. What procedure code(s) is (are) reported?

A. 49560, 49568

B. 49652

C. 49653

D. 49652, 49568

12. The patient is a 50 year-old gentleman who presented to the emergency room with signs and symptoms of acute appendicitis with possible rupture. He has been brought to the operating room. An infraumbilical incision was made which a 5-mm VersaStep™ trocar was inserted. A 5-mm 0-degree laparoscope was introduced. A second 5-mm trocar was placed suprapubically and a 12-mm trocar in the left lower quadrant. A window was made in the mesoappendix using blunt dissection with no rupture noted. The base of the appendix was then divided and placed into an Endo-catch bag and the 12-mm defect was brought out. Select the appropriate code for this procedure:

A. 44970

B. 44950

C. 44960

D. 44979

13. 45 year-old male is going to donate his kidney to his son. Operating ports where placed in standard position and the scope was inserted. Dissection of the renal artery and vein was performed isolating the kidney. The kidney was suspended only by the renal artery and vein as well as the ureter. A stapler was used to divide the vein just above the aorta and three clips across the ureter, extracting the kidney. This was placed on ice and sent to the recipient room. The correct CPT® code is:

A. 50543

B. 50547

C. 50300

D. 50320

14. 67 year-old female having urinary incontinence with intrinsic sphincter deficiency is having a cystoscopy performed with a placement of a sling. An incision was made over the mid urethra dissected laterally to urethropelvic ligament. Cystoscopy revealed no penetration of the bladder. The edges of the sling were weaved around the junction of the urethra and brought up to the suprapubic incision. A hemostat was then placed between the sling and the urethra, ensuring no tension. What CPT® code(s) is (are) reported?

A. 57288

B. 57287

C. 57288, 52000-51

D. 51992, 52000-51

15. 16 day-old male baby is in the OR for a repeat circumcision due to redundant foreskin that caused circumferential scarring from the original circumcision. Anesthetic was injected and an incision was made at base of the foreskin. Foreskin was pulled back and the excess foreskin was taken off and the two raw skin surfaces were sutured together to create a circumferential anastomosis. Select the appropriate code for this surgery:

A. 54150

B. 54160

C. 54163

D. 54164

16. 5 year-old female has a history of post void
    dribbling. She was found to have extensive labial
    adhesions, which have been unresponsive to topical
    medical management. She is brought to the
    operating suite in a supine position. Under general
    anesthesia the labia majora is retracted and the
    granulating chronic adhesions were incised midline
    both anteriorly and posteriorly. The adherent
    granulation tissue was excised on either side. What
    code should be used for this procedure?

    A. 58660

    B. 58740

    C. 57061

    D. 56441

17. The patient is a 64 year-old female who is undergoing a removal of a previously implanted Medtronic pain pump and catheter due to a possible infection. The back was incised; dissection was carried down to the previously placed catheter. There was evidence of infection with some fat necrosis in which cultures were taken. The intrathecal portion of the catheter was removed. Next the pump pocket was incised and the pump was dissected from the anterior fascia. A 7-mm Blake drain was placed in the pump pocket through a stab incision and secured to the skin with interrupted Prolene. The pump pocket was copiously irrigated with saline and closed in two layers. What are the CPT® and ICD-10-CM codes for this procedure?

A. 62365, 62350-51, T85.898A, Z46.2

B. 62360, 62355-51, T85.79XA

C. 62365, 62355-51, T85.79XA

D. 36590, I97.42, T85.898A

18. The patient is a 73 year-old gentleman who was noted to have progressive gait instability over the past several months. Magnetic resonance imaging demonstrated a ventriculomegaly. It was recommended that the patient proceed forward with right frontal ventriculoperitoneal shunt placement with Codman® programmable valve. What is the correct code for this surgery?

A. 62220

B. 62223

C. 62190

D. 62192

19. What is the CPT® code for the decompression of the median nerve found in the space in the wrist on the palmar side?

    A. 64704

    B. 64713

    C. 64721

    D. 64719

20. 2 year-old Hispanic male has a chalazion on both upper and lower lid of the right eye. He was placed under general anesthesia. With a #11 blade the chalazion was incised and a small curette was then used to retrieve any granulomatous material on both lids. What CPT® code should be used for this procedure?

A. 67801

B. 67805

C. 67800

D. 67808

21. 80 year-old patient is returning to the gynecologist's office for pessary cleaning. Patient offers no complaints. The nurse removes and cleans the pessary, vagina is swabbed with betadine, and pessary replaced. For F/U in 4 months. What CPT® and ICD-10-CM codes are reported for this service?

A. 99201, Z46.89

B. 99211, Z46.89

C. 99202, Z46.9

D. 99212, Z46.9

22. Patient was in the ER complaining of constipation with nausea and vomiting when taking Zovirax for his herpes zoster and Percocet for pain. His primary care physician came to the ER and admitted him to the hospital for intravenous therapy and management of this problem. His physician documented a detailed history, comprehensive examination and a medical decision making of moderate complexity. Which E/M service is reported?

A. 99285

B. 99284

C. 99221

D. 99222

23. 20 day-old infant was seen in the ER by the neonatologist admitting the baby to NICU for cyanosis and rapid breathing. The neonatologist performed intubation, ventilation management and a complete echocardiogram in the NICU and provided a report for the echocardiography which did indicate congenital heart disease. Select the correct codes for the physician service.

A. 99468-25, 93303-26

B. 99471-25, 31500, 94002, 93303-26

C. 99460-25, 31500, 94002, 93303-26

D. 99291-25, 93303-26

24. A 42 year-old with renal pelvis cancer receives general anesthesia for a laparoscopic radical nephrectomy. The patient has controlled type 2 diabetes otherwise no other co-morbidities. What is the correct CPT® and ICD-10-CM code for the anesthesia services?

A. 00860-P1, C64.9, E11.9

B. 00840-P3, C65.9, E11.9

C. 00862-P2, C65.9, E11.9

D. 00868-P2, C79.02, E11.9

25. A healthy 32 year-old with a closed distal radius fracture received monitored anesthesia care for an ORIF of the distal radius. What is the code for the anesthesia service?

A. 01830-P1

B. 01860-QS-P1

C. 01830-QS-P1

D. 01860-QS-G9-P1

26. A 10 month-old child is taken to the operating room for removal of a laryngeal mass. What is (are) the appropriate anesthesia code(s) to report?

A. 00320

B. 00326

C. 00320, 99100

D. 00326, 99100

27. A catheter is placed in the left common femoral artery which was directed into the right the external iliac (antegrade). Dye was injected and a right lower extremity angiogram was performed which revealed patency of the common femoral and profunda femoris. The catheter was then manipulated into the superficial femoral artery (retrograde) in which a lower extremity angiogram was performed which revealed occlusion from the popliteal to the tibioperoneal artery. What are the procedure codes that describe this procedure?

A. 36217, 75736-26

B. 36247, 75716-26

C. 36217, 75658-26

D. 36247, 75710-26

28. 56 year-old female is having a bilateral mammogram with computer aid detection conducted as a screening because the patient has had a previous cyst in the right breast. What radiological services are reported?

A. 77065 x 2

B. 77065, 77066

C. 77067

D. 77066

29. 63 year-old patient with bilateral ureteral obstruction presents to an outpatient facility for placement of a right and left ureteral stent along with an interpretation of a retrograde pyelogram. What codes should be reported?

A. 52332, 74000

B. 52332-50, 74420-26

C. 52005, 74420

D. 52005-50, 74425-26

30. Patient is coming in for a pathological examination for ischemia in the left leg. The first specimen is 1.5 cm of a single portion of arterial plaque taken from the left common femoral artery. The second specimen is 8.5 x 2.7 cm across x 1.5 cm in thickness of a cutaneous ulceration with fibropurulent material on the left leg. What surgical pathology codes should be reported for the pathologist?

A. 88304-26, 88302-26

B. 88305-26, 88304-26

C. 88307-26, 88305-26

D. 88309-26, 88307-26

31. During a craniectomy the surgeon asked for a consult and sent a frozen section of a large piece of tumor and sent it to pathology. The pathologist received a rubbery pinkish tan tissue measuring in aggregate 3 x 0.8 x 0.8 cm. The entire specimen is submitted in one block and also a gross and microscopic examination was performed on the tissue. The frozen section and the pathology report are sent back to the surgeon indicating that the tumor was a medulloblastoma. What CPT® code(s) will the pathologist report?

A. 80500

B. 88331-26, 88307-26

C. 80502

D. 88331-26, 88332-26, 88304-26

32. Physician orders a basic (80047) and comprehensive metabolic (80053) panels. Select the code(s) on how this is reported.

A. 80053, 80047

B. 80053

C. 80047, 82040, 82247, 82310, 84075, 84155, 84460, 84450

D. 80053, 82330

33. A 4 year-old is getting over his cold and will be getting three immunizations in the pediatrician's office by the nurse. The first vaccination administered is the Polio vaccine intramuscularly. The next vaccination is the live influenza (LAIV3) administered in the nose. The last vaccination is the Varicella (live) by subcutaneous route. What CPT® codes are reported for the administration and vaccines?

A. 90713, 90658, 90716, 90460, 90461 x 2

B. 90713, 90660, 90716, 90460, 90461 x 1

C. 90713, 90660, 90716, 90471, 90472, 90474

D. 90713, 90658, 90716, 90471, 90472, 90473

34. A patient with chronic renal failure is in the hospital being evaluated by his endocrinologist after just placing a catheter into the peritoneal cavity for dialysis. The physician is evaluating the dwell time and running fluid out of the cavity to make sure the volume of dialysate and the concentration of electrolytes and glucose are correctly prescribed for this patient. What code should be reported for this service?

A. 90935

B. 90937

C. 90947

D. 90945

35. An established patient had a comprehensive exam in which she has been diagnosed with dry eye syndrome in both eyes. The ophthalmologist measures the cornea for placement of the soft contact lens for treatment of this syndrome. What codes are reported by the ophthalmologist?

A. 92014-25, 92071-50

B. 99214-25, 92072-50

C. 92014-25, 92325-50

D. 92014-25, 92310-50

36. A patient who is a singer has been hoarse for a few months following an upper respiratory infection. She is in a voice laboratory to have a laryngeal function study performed by an otolaryngologist. She starts off with the acoustic testing first. Before she moves on to the aerodynamic testing she complains of throat pain and is rescheduled to come back to have the other test performed. What CPT® code is reported?

A. 92520

B. 92700

C. 92520-52

D. 92614-52

37. What is the difference between entropion and ectropion?

A. Entropion is the inward turning of the eyelid and ectropion is the outward turning of the eyelid.

B. Entropion is facial droop and ectropion is a facial spasm.

C. Entropion is the outward turning of the hands and ectropion is the inward turning of the hands.

D. Entropion inward turning of the feet and ectropion is the outward turning of the feet due to muscle disorder.

38. What is the full CPT® code description for 00846?

A. Anesthesia for intraperitoneal procedures in lower abdomen including laparoscopy; radical hysterectomy

B. Radical hysterectomy

C. Anesthesia for intraperitoneal procedures in lower abdomen including laparoscopy; not otherwise specified radical hysterectomy

D. Radical hysterectomy not otherwise specified

39. Ventral, umbilical, Spigelian and incisional are types of:

A. Surgical approaches

B. Hernias

C. Organs found in the digestive system

D. Cardiac catheterizations

40. Fracturing the acetabulum involves what area?

    A. Skull

    B. Shoulder

    C. Pelvis

    D. Leg

41. When a patient is having a tenotomy performed on the abductor hallucis muscle, where is this muscle located?

A. Foot

B. Upper Arm

C. Upper Leg

D. Hand

42. 44 year-old had a history of adenocarcinoma of the cervix on a conization in March 20XX who has been followed with twice-yearly endocervical curettages and Pap smears that were all negative for two years, per the recommendation of a GYN oncologist. Her Pap smear results from the last visit noted atypical glandular cells. In light of this, she underwent a colposcopy and the biopsy of the normal-appearing cervix on colposcopy was benign. The endocervical curettage was benign endocervical glands, and the endometrial sampling was benign endometrium. In light of the fact that she had had previous atypical glandular cells that led to diagnosis of adenocarcinoma and the concerns that this may have recurred, she had been recommended for a cone biopsy and fractional dilatation and curettage, which she is undergoing today. What ICD-10-CM code(s) should be reported?

A. R87.619, C53.9

B. C55

C. R87.619, Z85.41

D. Z12.4, Z85.41

43. Patient comes into see her primary care physician for a productive cough and shortness of breath. The physician takes a chest X-ray which indicates the patient has double pneumonia. Select the ICD-10-CM code(s) for this visit.

A. J18.9, R05, R06.2

B. R05, R06.2, J18.9

C. J18.9

D. J15.9

44. What is the correct way to code a patient having bradycardia due to Demerol that was correctly prescribed and properly administered?

A. T40.2X1A, R00.1

B. T40.2X3A, R00.1

C. R00.1, T40.2X5A

D. R00.1, T40.2X2A

45. Which statement is TRUE when reporting pregnancy codes (O00-O90A):

A. These codes can be used on the maternal and baby records.

B. These codes have sequencing priority over codes from other chapters.

C. Code Z33.1 should always be reported with these codes.

D. The seventh character assigned to these codes only indicate a complication during the pregnancy.

46. 66 year-old Medicare patient, who has a history of ulcerative colitis, presents for a colorectal cancer screening. The screening is performed via barium enema. What HCPCS Level II code is reported for this procedure?

A. G0104

B. G0105

C. G0120

D. G0121

47. What is PHI?

A. Physician-health care interchange

B. Private health insurance

C. Protected health information

D. Provider identified incident-to

48. What is NOT included in CPT® surgical package?

A. Typical postoperative follow-up care

B. One related Evaluation and Management service on the same date of the procedure

C. Returning to the operating room the next day for a complication resulting from the initial procedure

D. Evaluating the patient in the post-anesthesia recovery area

49. Which of the following is TRUE about reporting codes for diabetes mellitus?

A. If the type of diabetes mellitus is not documented in the medical record the default type is E11. - Type 2 diabetes mellitus.

B. When a patient uses insulin, Type 1 is always reported.

C. The age of the patient is a sole determining factor to report Type 1.

D. When assigning codes for diabetes and its associated condition(s), the code(s) from category E08-E13 are not reported as a primary code.

50. Which statement is TRUE for reporting external cause codes of morbidity (V00-Y99)?

A. All external cause codes do not require a seventh character.

B. Only report one external cause code to fully explain each cause.

C. Report code Y92.9 if the place of occurrence is not stated.

D. External cause codes should never be sequenced as a first-listed or primary code

51. PRE OP DIAGNOSIS: Left Breast Abnormal MMX or Palpable Mass; Other Disorders of Breast

PROCEDURE: Automated Stereotactic Biopsy Left Breast

FINDINGS: Lesion is located in the lateral region, just at or below the level of the nipple on the 90 degree lateral view. There is a subglandular implant in place. I discussed the procedure with the patient today including risks, benefits and alternatives. Specifically discussed was the fact that the implant would be displaced out of the way during this biopsy procedure. Possibility of injury to the implant was discussed with the patient. Patient has signed the consent form and wishes to proceed with the biopsy. The patient was placed prone on the stereotactic table; the left breast was then imaged from the inferior approach. The lesion of interest is in the anterior portion of the breast away from the implant which was displaced back toward the chest wall. After imaging was obtained and stereotactic guidance used to target coordinates for the biopsy, the left breast was prepped with Betadine. 1% lidocaine was injected subcutaneously for local anesthetic. Additional lidocaine with epinephrine was then injected through the indwelling needle. The SenoRx needle was then placed into the area of interest. Under stereotactic guidance we obtained 9 core biopsy samples using vacuum and cutting technique. The specimen radiograph confirmed representative sample of calcification was removed. The tissue marking clip was deployed into the biopsy cavity successfully. This was confirmed by final stereotactic digital image and confirmed by post core biopsy mammogram left breast. The clip is visualized projecting over the lateral anterior left breast in satisfactory position. No obvious calcium is visible on the final post core biopsy image in the area of interest. The patient tolerated the procedure well. There were no apparent complications. The biopsy site was dressed with Steri-Strips, bandage and ice pack in the usual manner. The patient did receive written and verbal post-biopsy instructions. The patient left our department in good condition.

IMPRESSION: 1. SUCCESSFUL STEREOTACTIC CORE BIOPSY OF LEFT BREAST CALCIFICATIONS.

2. SUCCESSFUL DEPLOYMENT OF THE TISSUE MARKING CLIP INTO THE BIOPSY CAVITY

3. PATIENT LEFT OUR DEPARTMENT IN GOOD CONDITION TODAY WITH POST-BIOPSY INSTRUCTIONS.

4. PATHOLOGY REPORT IS PENDING; AN ADDENDUM WILL BE ISSUED AFTER WE RECEIVE THE PATHOLOGY REPORT.

What is (are) the CPT® code(s)?

A. 19081

B. 19283

C. 19081, 19283

D. 19100, 19283

52. 53 year-old male is in the dermatologist's office for removal of 2 lesions located on his lower lip and nose. Lesions were identified and marked. The lower lip lesion of 4mm in size was shaved to the level of the superficial dermis. Utilizing a 3-mm punch, a biopsy was taken of the left supratip nasal area. What are the CPT® codes for these procedures?

A. 11100, 11101

B. 11310, 11100-59

C. 17000, 17003

D. 11440, 11000-59

53. 76 year-old has dermatochalasis on bilateral upper eyelids. A blepharoplasty will be performed on the eyelids. A lower incision line was marked at approximately 5 mm above the lid margin along the crease. Then using a pinch test with forceps the amount of skin to be resected was determined and marked. An elliptical incision was performed on the left eyelid and the skin was excised. In a similar fashion the same procedure was performed on the right eye. The wounds were closed with sutures. The correct CPT® code(s) is/are?

A. 15822, 15823-51

B. 15823-50

C. 15822-50

D. 15820-LT, 15820-RT

54. 42 year-old male has a frozen left shoulder. An arthroscope was inserted in the posterior portal in the glenohumeral joint. The articular cartilage was normal except for some minimal grade III-IV changes, about 5% of the humerus just adjacent to the rotator cuff insertion of the supraspinatus. The biceps was inflamed, not torn at all. The superior labrum was not torn at all, the labrum was completely intact. The rotator cuff was completely intact. An anterior portal was established high in the rotator interval. The rotator interval was very thick and contracted. Adhesions were destroyed with electrocautery and the Bovie. The superior glenohumeral ligament, the middle glenohumeral ligament and the tendinous portion of the subscapularis were released. The arthroscope was placed anteriorly, adhesions were destroyed and the shaver was used to debride some of the posterior capsule and the posterior capsule was released in its posterosuperior and then posteroinferior aspect. What CPT® code(s) is (are) reported?

A. 23450-LT

B. 23466-LT

C. 29805-LT, 29806-51-LT

D. 29825-LT

55. After adequate anesthesia was obtained the patient was turned prone in a kneeling position on the spinal table. A lower midline lumbar incision was made and the soft tissues divided down to the spinous processes. The soft tissues were stripped away from the lamina down to the facets and discectomies and laminectomies were then carried out at L3-4, L4-5 and L5-S1. Interbody fusions were set up for the lower three levels using the Danek allografts and augmented with structural autogenous bone from the iliac crest. The posterior instrumentation of a 5.5 mm diameter titanium rod was then cut to the appropriate length and bent to confirm to the normal lordotic curve. It was then slid immediately onto the bone screws and at each level compression was carried out as each of the two bolts were tightened so that the interbody fusions would be snug and as tight as possible. Select the appropriate CPT® codes for this visit?

A. 22612, 22614 x 2, 22842, 20938, 20930

B. 22533, 22534 x 2, 22842

C. 22630, 22632 x 2, 22842, 20938, 20930

D. 22554, 22632 x 2, 22842

56. PREOPERATIVE DIAGNOSIS: Displaced impacted Colles fracture, left distal radius and ulna.

POSTOPERATIVE DIAGNOSIS: Displaced impacted Colles fracture, left distal radius and ulna.

OPERATIVE PROCEDURE: Reduction with application of an external fixation system, left wrist fracture

FINDINGS: The patient is a 46 year-old right-hand-dominant female who fell off stairs 4 to 5 days ago sustaining an impacted distal radius fracture with possible intraarticular component and an associated ulnar styloid fracture. Today in surgery, fracture was reduced anatomically and an external fixation system was applied.

PROCEDURE: Under satisfactory general anesthesia, the fracture was manipulated and C-arm images were checked. The left upper extremity was prepped and draped in the usual sterile orthopedic fashion. Two small incisions were made over the second metacarpal and after removing soft tissues including tendinous structures out of the way, drawing was carried out and blunt-tipped pins were placed for the EBI external fixator. The frame was next placed and the site for the proximal pins was chosen. Small incision was made. Subcutaneous tissues were carried out of the way. The pin guide was placed and 2 holes were drilled and blunt-tipped pins placed. Fixator was assembled. C-arm images were checked. Fracture reduction appeared to be anatomic. Suturing was carried out where needed with 4-0 Vicryl interrupted subcutaneous and 4-0 nylon interrupted sutures. Sterile dressings were applied. Vascular supply was noted to be satisfactory. Final frame tightening was carried out. What CPT® code(s) is/are reported?

A. 25600-LT, 20692-51

B. 25605- LT, 20690-51

C. 25606-LT

D. 25607-LT

57. 79 year-old male with symptomatic bradycardia and syncope is taken to the Operating Suite where an insertion of a DDD pacemaker will be performed. After the anesthesiologist provided moderate sedation, the cardiologist performed a left subclavian venipuncture was carried out. A guide wire was passed through the needle, and the needle was withdrawn. A second subclavian venipuncture was performed, a second guide wire was passed and the second needle was withdrawn. An oblique incision in the deltopectoral area incorporating the wire exit sites. A subcutaneous pocket was created with the cautery on the pectoralis fascia. An introducer dilator was passed over the first wire and the wire and dilator were withdrawn. A ventricular lead was passed through the introducer, and the introducer was broken away in the routine fashion. A second introducer dilator was passed over the second guide wire and the wire and dilator were withdrawn. An atrial lead was passed through the introducer and the introducer was broken away in the routine fashion. Each of the leads were sutured down to the chest wall with two 2-0 silk sutures each, connected the leads to the generator, curled the leads, and the generator was placed in

the pocket. We assured hemostasis. We assured good position with the fluoroscopy. What CPT® code(s) is (are) reported by the cardiologist?

A. 33208

B. 33212

C. 33226

D. 33235, 71090-26

58. Patient has lung cancer in his upper right and middle lobes. Patient is in the operating suite to have a video-assisted thorascopy surgery (VATS). A 10-mm-zero-degree thoracoscope is inserted in the right pleural cavity through a port site placed in the ninth and seventh intercostal spaces. Lung was deflated. The tumor is in the right pleural. Both lobes were removed thorascopically. Port site closed. A chest tube was placed to suction and patient was sent to recovery in stable condition. Which CPT® code is reported for this procedure?

A. 32482

B. 32484

C. 32670

D. 32671

59. The patient is a 58 year-old white male, one month status post pneumonectomy. He had a post pneumonectomy empyema treated with a tunneled cuffed pleural catheter which has been draining the cavity for one month with clear drainage. He has had no evidence of a block or pleural fistula. Therefore a planned return to surgery results in the removal of the catheter. The correct CPT® code is:

A. 32440-78

B. 32035-58

C. 32036-79

D. 32552-58

60. This 67 year-old man presented with a history of progressive shortness of breath. He has had a diagnosis of a secundum atrioseptal defect for several years, and has had atrial fibrillation intermittently over this period of time. He was in atrial fibrillation when he came to the operating room, and with the patient cannulated and on bypass, the right atrium was then opened. A large 3 x 5 cm defect was noted at fossa ovalis, and this also included a second hole in the same general area. Both of these holes were closed with a single pericardial patch. What CPT® and ICD-10-CM codes are reported?

A. 33675, Q21.0

B. 33647, Q21.1, R06.02

C. 33645, Q21.2, R06.02

D. 33641, Q21.1

61. An 82 year-old female had a CAT scan which revealed evidence of a proximal small bowel obstruction. She was taken to the Operating Room where an elliptical abdominal incision was made, excising the skin and subcutaneous tissue. There were extensive adhesions along the entire length of the small bowel: the omentum and bowel were stuck up to the anterior abdominal wall. Time consuming, tedious and spending an extra hour to lysis the adhesions to free up the entire length of the gastrointestinal tract from the ligament to Treitz to the ileocolic anastomosis. The correct CPT® code is:

A. 44005

B. 44180-22

C. 44005-22

D. 44180-59

62. 55 year-old patient was admitted with massive gastric dilation. The endoscope was inserted with a catheter placement. The endoscope is passed through the cricopharyngeal muscle area without difficulty. Esophagus is normal, some chronic reflux changes at the esophagogastric junction noted. Stomach significant distention with what appears to be multiple encapsulated tablets in the stomach at least 20 to 30 of these are noted. Some of these are partially dissolved. Endoscope could not be engaged due to high grade narrowing in the pyloric channel, the duodenum was not examined. It seems to be a high grade outlet obstruction with a superimposed volvulus. A repeat examination is not planned at this time. What code should be used for this procedure?

A. 43246-52

B. 43241-52

C. 43235

D. 43191

63. The patient is a 78 year-old white female with morbid obesity that presented with small bowel obstruction. She had surgery approximately one week ago and underwent exploration, which required a small bowel resection of the terminal ileum and anastomosis leaving her with a large inferior ventral hernia. Two days ago she started having drainage from her wound which has become more serious. She is now being taken back to the operating room. Reopening the original incision with a scalpel, the intestine was examined and the anastomosis was reopened, excised at both ends, and further excision of intestine. The fresh ends were created to perform another end- to-end anastomosis. The correct procedure code is:

A. 44120-78

B. 44126-79

C. 44120-76

D. 44202-58

64. PREOPERATIVE DIAGNOSIS: Diverticulitis, perforated diverticula

POST OPERATIVE DIAGNOSIS: Diverticulitis, perforated diverticula

PROCEDURE: Hartmann procedure, which is a sigmoid resection with Hartmann pouch and colostomy.

DESCRIPTION OF THE PROCEDURE: Patient was prepped and draped in the supine position under general anesthesia. Prior to surgery patient was given 4.5 grams of Zosyn and Rocephin IV piggyback. A lower midline incision was made, abdomen was entered. Upon entry into the abdomen, there was an inflammatory mass in the pelvis and there was a large abscessed cavity, but no feces. The abscess cavity was drained and irrigated out. The left colon was immobilized, taken down the lateral perineal attachments. The sigmoid colon was mobilized. There was an inflammatory mass right at the area of the sigmoid colon consistent with a diverticulitis or perforation with infection. Proximal to this in the distal left colon, the colon was divided using a GIA stapler with 3.5 mm staples. The sigmoid colon was then mobilized using blunt dissection. The proximal rectum just distal to the inflammatory mass was divided using a GIA stapler with 3.5 mm staples. The mesentery of the sigmoid colon was then taken down and tied using two 0 Vicryl ties. Irrigation was again performed and the sigmoid colon was removed with inflammatory mass. The wall of the abscessed cavity that was next to the sigmoid colon where the inflammatory mass was, showed no leakage of stool, no gross perforation, most likely there is a small perforation in one of the diverticula in this region. Irrigation was again performed throughout the abdomen until totally clear. All excess fluid was removed. The distal descending colon was then brought out through a separate incision in the lower left quadrant area and a large 10 mm 10 French JP drain was placed into the abscessed cavity. The sigmoid colon or the colostomy site was sutured on the inside using interrupted 3-0 Vicryl to the peritoneum and then two sheets of film were placed into the intra- abdominal cavity. The fascia was closed using a running #1 double loop PDS suture and intermittently a #2 nylon retention suture was placed. The colostomy was matured using interrupted 3-0 chromic sutures. I palpated the colostomy; it was completely patent with no obstructions. Dressings were applied. Colostomy bag was applied. Which CPT® code should be used?

A. 44140

B. 44143

C. 44160

D. 44208

65. 5 year-old male with a history of prematurity was found to have a chordee due to congenital hypospadias. He presents for surgical management for a plastic repair in straightening the abnormal curvature. Under general anesthesia, bands were placed around the base of the penis and incisions were made degloving the penis circumferentially. The foreskin was divided in Byers flaps and the penile skin was reapproximated at the 12 o'clock position. Two Byers flaps were reapproximated, recreating a mucosal collar which was then criss-crossed and trimmed in the midline in order to accommodate median raphe reconstruction. This was reconstructed with use of a horizontal mattress suture. The shaft skin was then approximated to the mucosal collar with sutures correcting the defect. Which CPT® code should be used?

A. 54304

B. 54340

C. 54400

D. 54440

66. 22 year-old is 14 weeks pregnant and wants to terminate the pregnancy. She has consented for a D&E. She was brought to the operating room where MAC anesthesia was given. She was then placed in the dorsal lithotomy position and a weighted speculum was placed into her posterior vaginal vault. Cervix was identified and dilated. A 6.5-cm suction catheter hooked up to a suction evacuator was placed and products of conception were evacuated. A medium size curette was then used to curette her endometrium. There was noted to be a small amount of remaining products of conception in her left cornea. Once again the suction evacuator was placed and the remaining products of conception were evacuated. At this point she had a good endometrial curetting with no further products of conception noted. Which CPT® code should be used?

A. 59840

B. 59841

C. 59812

D. 59851

67. A 37 year-old female has menorrhagia and wants permanent sterilization. The patient was placed in Allen stirrups in the operating room. Under anesthesia the cervix was dilated and the hysteroscope was advanced to the endometrium into the uterine cavity. No polyps or fibroids were seen. The Novasure was used for endometrial ablation. A knife was then used to make an incision in the right lower quadrant and left lower quadrant with 5-mm trocars inserted under direct visualization with no injury to any abdominal contents. Laparoscopic findings revealed the uterus, ovaries and fallopian tubes to be normal. The appendix was normal as were the upper quadrants. Because of the patient's history of breast cancer and desire for no further children, it was decided to take out both the tubes and ovaries. This had been discussed with the patient prior to surgery. What are the codes for these procedures?

A. 58660, 58353-51

B. 58661, 58563-51

C. 58661, 58558-51

D. 58662, 58563-51

68. MRI reveals patient has cervical stenosis. It was determined he should undergo bilateral cervical laminectomy at C3 through C6 and fusion. The edges of the laminectomy were then cleaned up with a Kerrison and foraminotomies were done at C4, C5, and C6. The stenosis is central; a facetectomy is performed by using a burr. Nerve root canals were freed by additional resection of the facet, and compression of the spinal cord was relieved by removal of a tissue overgrowth around the foramen. Which CPT® code(s) is (are) used for this procedure?

A. 63045-50, 63048-50

B. 63020-50, 63035-50, 63035-50

C. 63015-50

D. 63045, 63048 x 2

69. An extracapsular cataract removal is performed on the right eye by manually using an iris expansion device to expand the pupil. A phacoemulsification unit was used to remove the nucleus and irrigation and aspiration was used to remove the residual cortex allowing the insertion of the intraocular lens. What CPT® code is reported?

A. 66985

B. 66984

C. 66982

D. 66983

70. An infant who has chronic otitis media in the right and left ears was placed under general anesthesia and a radial incision was made in the posterior quadrant of the left and right tympanic membranes. A large amount of mucoid effusion was suctioned and then a ventilating tube was placed in both ears. What CPT® and ICD-10-CM codes are reported?

A. 69436-50, H65.33

B. 69436-50, H66.43

C. 69433-50, H65.113

D. 69421-50, H65.33

71. 50 year-old patient is coming to see her primary care physician for hypertension. The patient also discusses with her physician that the OBGYN office had just told her that her Pap smear came back with an abnormal reading and is worried because her aunt had passed away with cervical cancer. The physician documents she spent 40 minutes face-to-face time with the patient, and 25 minutes of that time is giving counseling on the awareness, other screening procedures and treatment if it turns out to be cervical cancer. What E/M code(s) is (are) reported for this visit?

A. 99215

B. 99213, 99358

C. 99214, 99354

D. 99213

72. A patient was admitted yesterday to the hospital for possible gallstones. The following day the physician who admitted the patient performed a detailed history, a detailed exam and a medical decision making of low complexity. The physician tells her the test results have come back positive for gallstones and is recommending having a cholecystectomy. What code is reported for this evaluation and management service for the following day?

A. 99253

B. 99221

C. 99233

D. 99234

73. A patient came in to the ER with wheezing and a rapid heart rate. The ER physician documents a comprehensive history, comprehensive exam and medical decision of moderate complexity. The patient has been given three nebulizer treatments. The ER physician has decided to place him in observation care for the acute asthma exacerbation. The ER physician will continue examining the patient and will order additional treatments until the wheezing subsides. Select the appropriate code(s) for this visit.

A. 99284, 99219

B. 99219

C. 99284

D. 99235

74. A 6 month-old patient is administered general anesthesia to repair a cleft palate. What anesthesia code(s) is (are) reported for this procedure?

A. 00170, 99100

B. 00172

C. 00172, 99100

D. 00176

75. A 50 year-old female had a left subcutaneous mastectomy for cancer. She now returns for reconstruction which is done with a single TRAM flap. Right mastopexy is done for asymmetry. Select the anesthesia code for this procedure.

A. 00404

B. 00402

C. 00406

D. 00400

76. A patient is having knee replacement surgery. The surgeon requests that in addition to the general anesthesia for the procedure that the anesthesiologist also insert a continuous lumbar epidural infusion for postoperative pain management. The anesthesiologist performs postoperative management for two postoperative days.

A. 01400-AA, 62326, 01996 x 2

B. 01402-AA, 62327, 01966 x 2

C. 01402-AA, 62326, 01996 x 2

D. 01404-AA, 62327

77. 35 year-old male sees his primary care physician complaining of fever with chills, cough and congestion. The physician performs a chest X-ray taking lateral and AP views in his office. The physician interprets the X-ray views and the patient is diagnosed with walking pneumonia. Which CPT® code is reported for the chest X-rays performed in the office and interpreted by the physician?

A. 71020-26

B. 71030-26

C. 71020

D. 71010-26-TC

78. This gentleman has localized prostate cancer and has chosen to have complete transrectal ultrasonography performed for dosimetry purposes. Following calculation of the planned transrectal ultrasound, guidance was provided for percutaneous placement of 1-125 seeds. Select the appropriate codes for this procedure.

A. 55920, 76965-26

B. 55876, 76942-26

C. 55860, 76873-26

D. 55875, 76965-26

79. 76-year-old female had a ground level fall when she tripped over her dog earlier this evening in her apartment. The Emergency Department took X-rays of the left wrist in oblique and lateral views which revealed a displaced distal radius fracture, type I open left wrist. What radiological service and ICD-10-CM codes are reported?

A. 73100-26, S52.502B, W18.31XA, Y92.039

B. 73110-26, S52.602A, W18.31XA, Y92.039

C. 73115-26, S52.502A, W18.31XA, Y92.039

D. 73100-26, S52.602B, W18.31XA, Y92.039

80. 18 year-old female with a history of depression comes into the ER in a coma. The ER physician orders a drug screen on antidepressants, phenothiazines, and benzodiazepines. The lab performs a screening for single drug class using an immunoassay in a random access chemistry analyzer. Presence of antidepressants is found and a drug confirmation is performed to identify the particular antidepressant. What correct CPT® codes are reported?

A. 80307, 80338

B. 80305, 80338

C. 80306 x 3, 80332

D. 80307 x 3, 80333

81. A patient uses Topiramate to control his seizures. He comes in every two months to have a therapeutic drug testing performed to assess serum plasma levels of this medication. What lab code(s) is (are) reported for this testing?

A. 80305

B. 80375

C. 80201

D. 80306, 80375

82. Patient that is a borderline diabetic has been sent to the laboratory to have an oral glucose tolerance test. Patient drank the glucose and five blood specimens were taken every 30 to 60 minutes up to three hours to determine how quickly the glucose is cleared from the blood. What code(s) is (are) reported for this test?

A. 82947 x 5

B. 82946

C. 80422

D. 82951, 82952 x 2

83. A patient with severe asthma exacerbation has been admitted. The admitting physician orders a blood glass for oxygen saturation only. The admitting physician performs the arterial puncture drawing blood for a blood gas reading on oxygen saturation only. The physician draws it again in an hour to measure how much oxygen the blood is carrying. Select the codes for reporting this service.

A. 82805, 82805-51

B. 82810, 82810-91

C. 82803, 82803-51

D. 82805, 82805-90

84. A new patient is having a cardiovascular stress test done in his cardiologist's office. Before the test is started the physician documents a comprehensive history and exam and moderate complexity medical decision making. The physician will be supervising and interpreting the stress on the patient's heart during the test. What procedure codes are reported for this encounter?

A. 93015-26, 99204-25

B. 93016, 93018, 99204-25

C. 93015, 99204-25

D. 93018-26, 99204-25

85. A cancer patient is coming in to have a chemotherapy infusion. The physician notes the patient is dehydrated and will first administer a hydration infusion. The infusion time was 1 hour and 30 minutes. Select the code(s) that is (are) reported for this encounter?

A. 96360

B. 96360, 96361

C. 96365, 96366

D. 96422

86. A patient that has multiple sclerosis has been seeing a therapist for four visits. Today's visit the therapist will be performing a comprehensive reevaluation to determine the extent of progress. There was a revised plan assessing the changes in the patient's functional status. Initial profile was updated to reflect changes that affect future goals along with a revised plan of care. A total care of 30 minutes were spent in this re-evaluation. What CPT® and ICD-10-CM codes should be reported?

A. 97168, Z51.89, G35

B. 97164, Z56.89, G35

C. 97167, G35

D. 97163, Z56.9, G35

87. What is the term used for inflammation of the bone and bone marrow?

A. Chondromatosis

B. Osteochondritis

C. Costochondritis

D. Osteomyelitis

88. The root word trich/o means:

A. Hair

B. Sebum

C. Eyelid

D. Trachea

89. Complete this series: Frontal lobe, Parietal lobe, Temporal lobe, _____.

A. Medulla lobe

B. Occipital lobe

C. Middle lobe

D. Inferior lobe

90. A patient is having pyeloplasty performed to treat an uretero-pelvic junction obstruction. What is being performed?

A. Surgical repair of the bladder

B. Removal of the kidney

C. Cutting into the ureter

D. Surgical reconstruction of the renal pelvis

91. 27 year-old was frying chicken when an explosion of the oil had occurred and she sustained second-degree burns on her face (5%), third degree burns on both hands (5%). There was a total of 10 percent of the body surface that was burned. Select which ICD-10-CM codes are reported.

A. T20.20XA, T23.301A, T23.302A, T31.10, X10.2XXA, Y93.G3

B. T23.301A, T23.302A, T20.20XA, T31.11, X10.2XXA, Y93.G3

C. T23.301A, T23.302A, T20.20XA, T31.10, X10.2XXA, Y93.G3

D. T23.601A, T23.602A, T20.60XA, T31.10, X10.2XXA, Y93.G3

92. A patient that has cirrhosis of the liver just had an endoscopy performed showing hemorrhagic esophageal varices. The ICD-10-CM codes are reported:

A. I85.01, K74.69

B. I85.11, K74.60

C. K74.60, I85.11

D. I85.00, K74.69

93. 55 year-old-patient had a fracture of his left knee cap six months ago. The fracture has healed but he still has staggering gait in which he will be going to physical therapy. What ICD-10-CM codes are reported?

A. S82.002A, R26.81

B. R26.0, S82.002A

C. S82.092S, R26.0

D. R26.0, S82.002S

94. Which statement is TRUE about Z codes:

A. Z codes are never reported as a primary code.

B. Z codes are only reported with injury codes.

C. Z codes may be used either as a primary code or a secondary code.

D. Z codes are always reported as a secondary code.

95. Patient with corneal degeneration is having a cornea transplant. The donor cornea had been previously prepared by punching a central corneal button with a guillotine punch. This had been stored in Optisol GS. It was gently rinsed with BSS Plus solution and was then transferred to the patient's eye on a Paton spatula and sutured with 12 interrupted 10-0 nylon sutures. Select the HCPCS Level II code for the corneal tissue.

A. V2790

B. V2785

C. V2628

D. V2799

96. The patient presents to the office for an injection. Joint prepped using sterile technique. Muscle group location: gluteus maximus. Sterilely injected with 40 mg of Kenalog-10, 2 cc Marcaine and 2 cc lidocaine 2%. Sterile bandage applied. Choose the HCPCS Level II code for this treatment.

A. J3301 x 4

B. J3301

C. J3300 x 40

D. J3300

97. Which of the following is an example of electronic data?

A. A digital X-ray

B. An explanation of benefits

C. An advance beneficiary notice

D. A written prescription

98. Which of the following health plans does not fall under HIPAA?

A. Medicaid

B. Medicare

C. Workers' compensation

D. Private plans

99. Guidelines from which of the following code sets are included as part of the code set requirements under HIPAA?

A. CPT® Category III codes

B. ICD-10-CM

C. HCPCS Level II

D. ADA Dental Codes

100.   Which of the following is an example of a case in which a diabetes-related problem exists and the code for diabetes is never sequenced first?

A. If the patient has an underdose of insulin due to an insulin pump malfunction.

B. If the patient is being treated for secondary diabetes.

C. If the patient is being treated for Type 2 diabetes and uses insulin.

D. If the patient is diabetic with an associated condition.

101.   Patient has basal cell carcinoma on his upper back. A map was prepared to correspond to the area of skin where the excisions of the tumor will be performed using Mohs micrographic surgery technique. There were three tissue blocks that were prepared for cryostat, sectioned, and removed in the first stage. Then a second stage had six tissue blocks which were also cut and stained for microscopic examination. The entire base and margins of the excised pieces of tissue were examined by the surgeon. No tumor was identified after the final stage of the microscopically controlled surgery. What procedure codes are reported?

A. 17313, 17314, 17314

B. 17313, 17315

C. 17260, 17313, 17314

D. 17313, 17314, 17315

102.   45 year-old male is in outpatient surgery to excise a basal cell carcinoma of the right nose and have reconstruction with an advancement flap. The 1.2 cm lesion with an excised diameter of 1.5 cm was excised with a 15-blade scalpel down to the level of the subcutaneous tissue, totaling a primary defect of 1.8 cm. Electrocautery was used for hemostasis. An adjacent tissue transfer of 3 sq cm was taken from the nasolabial fold and was advanced into the primary defect. Which CPT® code(s) is (are) reported?

A. 14060

B. 11642, 14060

C. 11642, 15115

D. 15574

103.   24 year-old patient had an abscess by her vulva which burst. She has developed a soft tissue infection caused by gas gangrene. The area was debrided of necrotic infected tissue. All of the pus was removed and irrigation was performed with a liter of saline until clear and clean. The infected area was completely drained and the wound was packed gently with sterile saline moistened gauze and pads were placed on top of this. The correct CPT® code is:

A. 56405

B. 10061

C. 11004

D. 11042

104.   76 year-old female had a recent mammographic and ultrasound abnormality in the 6 o'clock position of the left breast. She underwent core biopsies which showed the presence of a papilloma. The plan now is for needle localization with excisional biopsy to rule out occult malignancy. After undergoing preoperative needle localization with hookwire needle injection with methylene blue, the patient was brought to the operating room and was placed on the operating room table in the supine position where she underwent laryngeal mask airway (LMA) anesthesia. The left breast was prepped and draped in a sterile fashion. A radial incision was then made in the 6 o'clock position of the left breast corresponding to the tip of the needle localizing wire. Using blunt and sharp dissection, we performed a generous excisional biopsy around the needle localizing wire including all of the methylene blue-stained tissues. The specimen was then submitted for radiologic confirmation followed by permanent section pathology. Once hemostasis was assured, digital palpation of the depths of the wound field failed to reveal any other palpable abnormalities. At this point, the wound was closed in 2 layers with 3-0

Vicryl and 5-0 Monocryl. Steri-Strips were applied. Local anesthetic was infiltrated for postoperative analgesia. What CPT® and ICD-10-CM codes describe this procedure?

A. 19100, N63

B. 19285, C50.912

C. 19120, R92.8

D. 19125, D24.2

105.   The patient is a 66 year-old female who
presents with Dupuytren's disease in the right palm
and ring finger. This results in a contracture of the
ring digit MP joint. She is having a subtotal palmar
fasciectomy for Dupuytren's disease right ring digit
and palm. An extensive Brunner incision was then
made beginning in the proximal palm and
extending to the ring finger PIP crease. This
exposed a large pretendinous cord arising from the
palmar fascia extending distally over the flexor
tendons of the ring finger. The fascial attachments
to the flexor tendon sheath were released. At the
level of the metacarpophalangeal crease, one band
arose from the central pretendinous cord-one
coursing toward the middle finger. The digital nerve
was identified, and this diseased fascia was also
excised. What procedure code(s) is (are) used?

A. 26123-RT, 26125-F7

B. 26121-RT

C. 26035-RT

D. 26040-RT

106.   This is a 32 year-old female who presents today with sacroiliitis. On the physical exam there was pain on palpation of the left and right sacroiliac joint and fluoroscopic guidance was done for the needle positioning. Then 80 mg of Depo-Medrol and 1 mL of bupivacaine at 0.5% was injected into the left and right sacroiliac joint with a 22 gauge needle. The patient was able to walk from the exam room without difficulty. Follow up will be as needed. The correct CPT® code(s) is (are):

A. 20611

B. 27096-50, 77012

C. 27096-50

D. 27096, 27096-51, 77012

107. PREOPERATIVE DIAGNOSIS: Medial meniscus tear, right knee

POSTOPERATIVE DIAGNOSIS: Medial meniscus tear, extensive synovitis with an impingement medial synovial plica, right knee

TITLE OF PROCEDURE: Diagnostic operative arthroscopy, partial medial meniscectomy and synovectomy, right knee. The patient was brought to the operating room, placed in the supine position after which he underwent general anesthesia. The right knee was then prepped and draped in the usual sterile fashion. The arthroscope was introduced through an anterolateral portal, interim portal created anteromedially. The suprapatellar pouch was inspected. The findings on the patella and the femoral groove were as noted above. An intra-articular shaver was introduced to debride the loose fibrillated articular cartilage from the medial patellar facet. The hypertrophic synovial scarring between the patella and the femoral groove was debrided. The hypertrophic impinging medial synovial plica was resected. The hypertrophic synovial scarring overlying the intercondylar notch and lateral compartment was debrided. The medial compartment was inspected. An upbiting basket was introduced to transect the base of the degenerative posterior horn flap tear. This was removed with a grasper. The meniscus was then further contoured and balanced with an intra-articular shaver, reprobed and found to be stable. The cruciate ligaments were probed, palpated and found to be intact. The lateral compartment was then inspected. The lateral meniscus was probed and found to be intact. The loose fibrillated articular cartilage along the lateral tibial plateau was debrided with the intra-articular shaver. The knee joint was then thoroughly irrigated with the arthroscope. The arthroscope was then removed. Skin portals were closed with 3-0 nylon sutures. A sterile dressing was applied. The patient was then awakened and sent to the recovery room in stable condition. What CPT® and ICD-10-CM codes should be reported?

A. 29880-RT, M23.203, M65.80, M94.261, M22.41

B. 29881-RT, M23.211, M65.861, M94.261, M22.41

C. 29881-RT, M23.221, M65.861, M94.261, M22.41

D. 29880-RT, 29877-59-RT, M23.621, M65.80, M94.261, M22.41

108.   A 61 year-old gentleman with a history of a fall while intoxicated suffered a blow to the forehead and imaging revealed a posteriorly displaced odontoid fracture. The patient was taken into the Operating Room, and placed supine on the operating room table. Under mild sedation, the patient was placed in Gardner-Wells tongs and gentle axial traction under fluoroscopy was performed to gently try to reduce the fracture. It did reduce partially without any change in the neurologic examination. More manipulation would be necessary and it was decided to intubate and use fiberoptic technique. The anterior neck was prepped and draped and an incision was made in a skin crease overlying the C4-C5 area. Using hand-held retractors, the ventral aspect of the spine was identified and the C2-C3 disk space was identified using lateral fluoroscopy. Using some pressure upon the ventral aspect of the C2 body, we were able to achieve a satisfactory reduction of the fracture. Under direct AP and lateral fluoroscopic guidance, a Kirschner wire was advanced into the C2 body through the fracture line and into the odontoid process. This was then drilled, and a 42 millimeter cannulated lag screw was advanced

through the C2 body into the odontoid process.

What procedure code is reported?

A. 22505

B. 22326

C. 22315

D. 22318

109.   The patient is a 51 year-old gentleman who has end-stage renal disease. He was in the OR yesterday for a revision of his AV graft. The next day the patient had complications of the graft failing. The patient was back to the operating room where an open thrombectomy was performed on both sides getting good back bleeding, good inflow. Select the appropriate code for performing the procedure in a post-operative period:

A. 36831-76

B. 36831

C. 36831-78

D. 36831-58

110.   The patient is a 77 year-old white female who has been having right temporal pain and headaches with some visual changes and has a sed rate of 51. She is scheduled for a temporal artery biopsy to rule out temporal arteritis. A Doppler probe was used to isolate the temporal artery and using a marking pen the path of the artery was drawn. Lidocaine 1% was used to infiltrate the skin, and using a 15 blade scalpel the skin was opened in the preauricular area and dissected down to the subcutaneous tissue where the temporal artery was identified in its bed. It was a medium size artery and we dissected it out for a length of approximately 4 cm with some branches. The ends were ligated with 4-0 Vicryl, and the artery was removed from its bed and sent to Pathology as specimen. What CPT® code is reported?

A. 37609

B. 37605

C. 36625

D. 37799

111.   50 year-old female has recurrent lymphoma in the axilla. Ultrasound was used to localize the lymph node in question for needle guidance. An 11 blade scalpel was used to perform a small dermatotomy. An 18 x 10 cm Biopence needle was advanced through the dermatotomy to the periphery of the lymph node. A total of 4 biopsy specimens were obtained. Two specimens were placed an RPMI and 2 were placed in formalin and sent to laboratory. The correct CPT® code(s) is (are):

A. 10022

B. 38500, 77002-26

C. 38505, 76942-26

D. 38525, 76942-26

112.　　Patient is going into the OR for an appendectomy with a ruptured appendicitis. Right lower quadrant transverse incision was made upon entry to the abdomen. In the right lower quadrant there was a large amount of pus consistent with a right lower quadrant abscess. Intraoperative cultures anaerobic and aerobic were taken and sent to microbiology for evaluation. Irrigation of the pus was performed until clear. The base of the appendix right at the margin of the cecum was perforated. The mesoappendix was taken down and tied using 0-Vicryl ties and the appendix fell off completely since it was already ruptured with tissue paper thin membrane at the base. There was no appendiceal stump to close or to tie, just an opening into the cecum; therefore, the appendiceal opening area into the cecum was tied twice using figure of 8 Vicryl sutures. Omentum flap was tacked over this area and anchored in place using interrupted 3-0 Vicryl sutures to secure the repair. What CPT® and ICD-10-CM codes are reported?

A. 44950, K35.89

B. 44960, 49905, K35.3

C. 44950, 49905-51, K35.2

D. 44970, K37

113.   15 year-old female is to have a tonsillectomy performed for chronic tonsillitis and hypertrophied tonsils. A McIver mouth gag was put in place and the tongue was depressed. The nasopharynx was digitalized. No significant adenoid tissue was felt. The tonsils were then removed bilaterally by dissection. The uvula was a huge size because of edema, a part of this was removed and the raw surface over-sewn with 3-0 chromic catgut. Which CPT® code(s) is (are) reported?

A. 42821

B. 42825, 42104-51

C. 42826, 42106-51

D. 42842

114.   34 year-old male developed a ventral hernia when lifting a 60 pound bag. The patient is in surgery for a ventral herniorrhaphy. The abdomen was entered through a short midline incision revealing the fascial defect. The hernia sac and contents were able to easily be reduced and a large plug of mesh was placed into the fascial defect. The edge of the mesh plug was sutured to the fascia. What procedure code(s) is (are) reported?

A. 49560

B. 49561, 49568

C. 49652

D. 49560, 49568

115.   25 year-old female in the OR for ectopic pregnancy. Once the trocars were place a pneumoperitoneum was created and the laparoscope introduced. The left fallopian tube was dilated and was bleeding. The left ovary was normal. The uterus was of normal size, shape and contour. The right ovary and tube were normal. Due to the patient's body habitus the adnexa could not be visualized to start the surgery. At this point the laparoscopic approach was terminated. The pneumoperitoneum was deflated, and trocar sites were sutured closed. The trocars and laparoscopic instruments had been removed. Open surgery was performed incising a previous transverse scar from a cesarean section. The gestation site was bleeding and all products of conception and clots were removed. The left tube was grasped, clamped and removed in its entirety and passed off to pathology. What code(s) is (are) reported for this procedure?

A. 59150, 59120

B. 59151

C. 59121

D. 59120

116.   23 year-old who is pregnant at 39-weeks and 3 days is presenting for a low transverse cesarean section. An abdominal incision is made and was extended superiorly and inferiorly with good visualization of the bladder. The bladder blade was then inserted and the lower uterine segment incised in a transverse fashion with the scalpel. The bladder blade was removed and the infant's head delivered atraumatically. The nose and mouth were suctioned with the bulb suction trap and the cord doubly clamped and cut. The placenta was then removed manually. What CPT® and ICD-10-CM codes are reported for this procedure?

A. 59610, O34.211, Z37.0, Z3A.39

B. 59510, O64.1XX0, Z37.0, Z3A.39

C. 59514, O82, Z37.0, Z3A.39

D. 59515, O82, Z37.0, Z3A.39

117.   55 year-old female has a symptomatic rectocele. She had been admitted and taken to the main OR. An incision is made in the vagina into the perineal body (central tendon of the perineum). Dissection was carried underneath posterior vaginal epithelium all the way over to the rectocele. Fascial tissue was brought together with sutures creating a bridge and the rectocele had been reduced with good support between the vagina and rectum. What procedure code should be reported?

A. 45560

B. 57284

C. 57250

D. 57240

118.   A craniectomy is being performed on a patient who has Chiari malformation. Once the posterior inferior scalp was removed a C-1 and a partial C-2 laminectomy was then performed. The right cerebellar tonsil was dissected free of the dorsal medulla and a gush of cerebrospinal fluid gave good decompression of the posterior fossa content. Which CPT® code is reported?

A. 61322

B. 61345

C. 61343

D. 61458

119.   Under fluoroscopic guidance an injection of a combination of steroid and analgesic agent is performed on T2-T3, T4-T5, T6-T7 and T8-T9 on the left side into the paravertebral facet joints. The procedure was performed for pain due to thoracic root lesions. What are the procedure codes?

A. 64479, 64480x3, 77003

B. 64490, 64491, 64492x2, 77003

C. 64520x4, 77003

D. 64490, 64491, 64492

120.   An entropion repair is performed on the left lower eyelid in which undermining was performed with scissors of the inferior lid and inferior temporal region. Deep sutures were used to separate the eyelid margin outwardly along with stripping the lateral tarsus to provide firm approximation of the lower lid to the globe. The correct CPT® code is:

A. 67914-E4

B. 67924-E2

C. 67921-E2

D. 67917-E1

121.   The patient is here to follow up on her atrial fibrillation. Her primary care physician is not in the office. She will be seen by the partner physician that is also in the same group practice. No new problems. A problem focused history is performed. An expanded problem focused physical exam is documented with the following, Blood pressure is 110/64. Pulse is regular at 72. Temp is 98.6F Chest is clear. Cardiac normal sinus rhythm. Medical making decision is straightforward. Diagnosis: Atrial fibrillation, currently stable. What E/M code is reported for this service?

A. 99201

B. 99202

C. 99212

D. 99213

122.   Documentation of a new patient in a doctor's office setting supports a detailed history in which there are four elements for an extended history of present illness (HPI), three elements for an extended review of systems (ROS) and a pertinent Past, Family, Social History (PFSH). There is a detailed examination of six body areas and organ systems. The medical making decision making is of high complexity. Which E/M service supports this documentation?

A. 99205

B. 99204

C. 99203

D. 99202

123.   A 2 year-old is brought to the ER by EMS for near drowning. EMS had gotten a pulse. The ER physician performs endotracheal intubation, blood gas, and a central venous catheter placement. The ER physician documents a total time of 30 minutes on this critical infant in which the physician already subtracted the time for the other billable services. Select the E/M service and procedures to report for the ER physician?

A. 99291-25, 36555, 31500

B. 99291-25, 36556, 31500, 82803

C. 99285-25, 36556, 31500, 82803

D. 99475-25, 36556

124.   2 year-old is coming in with his mom to see the pediatrician for fever, sore throat, and pulling of the ears. The physician performs an expanded problem focused history. An expanded problem focused exam. A strep culture was taken for the pharyngitis and came back positive for strep throat. A diagnosis was also made of the infant having acute otitis media with effusion in both ears. The medical decision making was of moderate complexity with the giving of a prescription. What CPT® and ICD-10-CM codes are reported?

A. 99212, J02.9, H66.93

B. 99213, J02.0 H65.93

C. 99212, J02.0 H65.193

D. 99213, J02.0 H65.193

125. A very large lipoma is removed from the chest measuring 8 sq. cm and the defect is 12.2 cm requiring a layered closure with extensive undermining. MAC is performed by a medically directed Certified Registered Nurse Anesthetist (CRNA). Code the anesthesia service.

A. 00400-QX-QS

B. 00400-QS

C. 00300-QS

D. 00300-QX-QS

126.   PREOPERATIVE DIAGNOSIS: Multivessel coronary artery disease.

POSTOPERATIVE DIAGNOSIS: Multivessel coronary artery disease.

NAME OF PROCEDURE: Coronary artery bypass graft x 3, left internal mammary artery to the LAD, saphenous vein graft to the obtuse marginal, saphenous vein graft to the diagonal. The patient is placed on heart and lung bypass during the procedure. Anesthesia time: 6:00 PM to 12:00 AM Surgical time: 6:15 PM to 11:30 PM What is the correct anesthesia code and anesthesia time?

A. 00567, 6 hours

B. 00566, 6 hours

C. 00567, 5 hours and 30 minutes

D. 00566, 5 hours and 30 minutes

127.   A CT density study is performed on a post-menopausal female to screen for osteoporosis. Today's visit the bone density study will be performed on the spine. Which CPT® code is reported?

A. 77075

B. 77080

C. 77078

D. 72081

128.   The patient is 15-weeks pregnant with twins coming back to her obstetrician to have a transabdominal ultrasound performed to reassess anatomic abnormalities of both fetuses that were previously demonstrated in the last ultrasound. What ultrasound code(s) is (are) reported?

A. 76815

B. 76816, 76816-59

C. 76801, 76802

D. 76805, 76810

129.   67 year-old female fractured a port-a-cath surgically placed a year ago. Under sonographic guidance a needle was passed into the right common femoral vein. The loop snare was positioned in the right atrium where a portion of the fractured catheter was situated. The catheter crossed the atrioventricular valve with the remaining aspect of the catheter in the ventricle. A pigtail catheter was then utilized to loop the catheter and pull the catheter tip into the inferior vena cava. The catheter was then snared and pulled through the right groin removed in its entirety. What CPT® and ICD-10-CM codes are reported?

A. 37200, T81.509D

B. 37197, T82.514A

C. 37193, T80.219A

D. 37217, T88.8XXA

130.   3 year-old woman with ascites consented to a procedure to withdraw fluid from the abdominal cavity. Ultrasonic guidance was used for guiding the needle placement for the aspiration. What CPT® codes should be used?

A. 49083

B. 49180, 76942-26

C. 49082, 77002-26

D. 49180, 76998-26

131.   Cells were taken from amniotic fluid for analyzation of the chromosomes for possible Down's syndrome. The geneticist performs the analysis with two G-banded karyotypes analyzing 30 cells. Select the lab code(s) for reporting this service.

A. 88248

B. 88267, 88280, 88285

C. 88273, 88280, 88291

D. 88262, 88285

132.   Sperm is being prepared through a washing
           method to get it ready for the insemination of five
           oocytes for fertilization by directly injecting the
           sperm into each oocyte. Choose the CPT® codes to
           report this service.

A. 89257, 89280

B. 89260, 89280

C. 89261, 89280

D. 89260, 89268

133.   A pathologist performs a comprehensive consultation and report after reviewing a patient's records and specimens from another facility. The correct CPT® code to report this service is:

A. 88325

B. 99244

C. 88323

D. 88329

134.   Patient with hemiparesis on the dominant side due to having a CVA lives at home alone and has a therapist at his home site to evaluate meal preparation for self-care. The therapist observes the patient's functional level of performing kitchen management activities within safe limits. The therapist then teaches meal preparation using one handed techniques along with adaptive equipment to handle different kitchen appliances. The total time spent on this visit was 45 minutes. Report the CPT® and ICD-10-CM codes for this encounter.

A. 97530 x 3, I67.89, G81.91

B. 97535 x 3, G81.90, I69.959

C. 97530 x 3, I69.959, I67.89

D. 97535 x 3, I69.959

135.   10 year-old patient had a recent placement of a cochlear implant. She and her family see an audiologist to check the pressure and determine the strength of the magnet. The transmitter, microphone and cable are connected to the external speech processor and maximum loudness levels are determined under programming computer control. Which CPT® code should be used?

A. 92601

B. 92603

C. 92604

D. 92562

136.   A cardiologist pediatrician sends a four week-old baby to an outpatient facility to have an echocardiogram. The baby has been having rapid breathing. He is sedated and a probe is placed on the chest wall and images are taken through the chest wall. A report is generated and sent to the pediatrician. The interpretation of the report by the pediatrician reveals the baby has an atrial septal defect. Choose the CPT® code the cardiologist pediatrician should report.

A. 93303

B. 93315-26

C. 93303-26

D. 93315

137.   Glomerulonephritis is an inflammation affecting which system?

A. Digestive

B. Nervous

C. Urinary

D. Cardiovascular

138.   When a patient has fractured the proximal end of his humerus, where is the fracture located?

A. Upper end of the arm

B. Lower end of the leg

C. Upper end of the leg

D. Lower end of the arm

139.   What is another term for when a physician performs a reduction on a displaced fracture?

A. Casting

B. Manipulation

C. Skeletal traction

D. External fixation

140.   What does oligospermia mean?

A. Presence of blood in the semen

B. Deficiency of sperm in semen

C. Having sperm in urine

D. Formation of spermatozoa

141.   Thoracentesis is removing fluid or air from

the:

A. Lung

B. Chest cavity

C. Thoracic vertebrae

D. Heart

142.   An angiogram is a study to look inside:

A. Female Reproductive System

B. Urinary System

C. Blood Vessels

D. Breasts

143.   Which types of joints are considered synovial?

A. Suture joint, medial joint, and articulation joint

B. Ball-and-socket joint, hinge joint, and saddle point

C. Pivot joint, talus joint, and cranial joint

D. Ball-and-socket joint, nasal joint, and elevation joint

144.   Patient is going back to the OR for a re-exploration L5-S1 laminectomy for a presumed cerebrospinal fluid leak following a decompression procedure. A small partial laminectomy was slightly extended, however revealed no real evidence of leak. Valsalva maneuver was performed several times, no evidence of leak. There was a hematoma, which was drained. What ICD-10-CM code(s) is (are) reported by the physician?

A. G96.0

B. G97.61

C. G96.8

D. G96.0, T81.4XXA

145.   A patient that has hypertensive heart disease with congestive heart failure is coded:

A. I11.0, I50.9

B. I13.0

C. I13.0, I11.0, I50.9

D. I50.9, I11.0

146.   10 year-old-male sustained a Colles' fracture in which the pediatrician performs an application of short arm fiberglass cast. Select the HCPCS Level II code that is reported.

A. Q4012

B. A4580

C. A4570

D. Q4024

147.   35 year-old-female is getting a
Levonorgestrel implant system with supplies. The
HCPCS Level II code is:

A. S4989

B. J7306

C. A4264

D. J7301

148.   Local Coverage Determinations (LCD) are published to give providers information on which of the following?

A. Information on modifier use with procedure codes

B. CPT® codes that are bundled

C. Fee schedule information listed by CPT® code

D. Reasonable and necessary conditions of coverage for an item or service

149.   Which place of service code should be reported on the physician's claim for a surgical procedure performed in an ASC?

A. 21

B. 22

C. 24

D. 11

150.   If an ST elevation myocardial infarction (STEMI) converts to a non ST elevation myocardial infarction (NSTEMI) due to thrombolytic therapy, how is it reported, according to ICD-10-CM guidelines?

A. As unspecified AMI

B. As a subendocardial AMI

C. As STEMI

D. As a NSTEMI

ANSWER KEY & FULL RATIONALE

1. **C. 11626,12044-51**

   According to CPT® guidelines "Repair of an excision of a malignant lesion requiring intermediate or complex closure should be reported separately". The intermediate repair code is reported because it was a layered closure.

2. **C. 11044**

   Debridement is not being performed on an open fracture/open dislocation eliminating multiple choice answer B. The ulcer was debrided all the way to the bone of the foot, making multiple choice answer C, the correct procedure.

3. **D. 99283-25, 12053, 12034-59**

   To start narrowing your choices down, the hand and foot were closed with adhesive strips. The Section Guidelines in the CPT® manual for Repair (Closure) states: "Wound closure utilizing adhesive strips as the sole repair material

should be coded using the appropriate E/M
code." Eliminating multiple choice answers A
and B. The lacerations on the face are
intermediate repairs, because debridement and
glass debris was removed. The guidelines in the
CPT® codebook for Repair (Closure) states:
"Single-layer closure of heavily contaminated
wounds that have required extensive cleaning
or removal of particulate matter also
constitutes intermediate repair." Eliminating
multiple choice answer C. The intermediate
repair of the lacerations to the face totaled 6 cm
(12053). The right arm and left leg had cuts
measuring 5 cm each which totaled 10 cm
requiring intermediate repair (12034).

4. C. 21931, D17.1
The mass growing turned out to be a lipoma
found in the subcutaneous tissue of the flank. In
the ICD-10-CM Alphabetic Index, look for
Lipoma/subcutaneous/trunk. You are referred
to code D17.1, eliminating multiple choice
answers A and D. Because the 4 cm tumor was

found in the subcutaneous tissue code 21931 is the correct CPT® code to report.

5. A. 25628-RT

    Patient had an open reduction, meaning an incision was made to get to the fracture, eliminating multiple choice answer B. The fracture site was the scaphoid of the wrist (carpal), eliminating multiple choices C and D.

6. D. 27485-50

    Your keywords in the scenario to narrow your choices down to code 27485 are: "distal femur," "genu valgum," and "hemiepiphysiodesis."

7. C. 36561, 77001-26

    Patient is having an Infuse-A-Port put in his chest to receive chemotherapy. The subclavian vein (central venous) is being tunneled for the access device, eliminating multiple choices A and D. The patient had a subcutaneous pocket created to insert the power port, eliminating multiple choice answer B. Code 77001 reports fluoroscopic guidance for a central venous access device. Modifier 26 denotes the professional service.

8. A. 32557

    The drainage of fluid from the pleural cavity was performed via needle (percutaneous) with insertion of an indwelling catheter to drain the fluid, eliminating multiple choice answers B and D. The procedure was performed under ultrasound guidance, eliminating multiple choice answer C.

9. B. 35301, 35390

    The procedure involved removing plaque and the vessel lining from the carotid artery through a neck incision, eliminating multiple choice answers C and D. This was a re-operation (35390), as the original surgery was performed a year ago.

10. **B. 47562, K81.1**

   One way to narrow down your choices is by the diagnosis. The patient has chronic cholecystitis. In the ICD-10-CM Alphabetic Index, look for Cholecystitis/chronic, referring you to code K81.1. Verify code in the Tabular List for accuracy. This eliminates multiple choice A and C. The patient had a laparoscopic cholecystectomy, eliminating multiple choice answer D.

11. **B. 49652**

   The patient is having a laparoscopic ventral hernia repair, eliminating multiple choice answer A. The hernia is not documented as being incarcerated or strangulated, eliminating multiple choice answer C. A parenthetical note under the code description for 49652 indicates that a mesh insertion (49568) is not reported with this code when performed; eliminating multiple choice answer D.

12. A. 44970

Patient is having the surgery performed by a laparoscope, eliminating multiple choice answers B and C. The surgical procedure performed was an appendectomy, eliminating multiple choice D.

13. B. 50547

This is a surgical laparoscopic procedure for removing the kidney (nephrectomy), eliminating multiple choice answers C and D. The whole kidney was taken out from a donor and put on ice (cold preservation), eliminating multiple choice answer A.

14. A. 57288

Removal or revision of the sling is not being performed, eliminating multiple choice answer B. The procedure was an open surgery, eliminating multiple choice answer D. Cystoscopy procedure code is a separate procedure. According to CPT® Surgery guidelines, the codes designated as a "separate procedure" should not be reported in addition to the code for the total procedure or service of which it is considered an integral component." Meaning that the cystoscopy is included with the sling operation procedure because it was performed in the same surgical session.

15. C. 54163

The physician is not incising the membrane that attaches the foreskin to the glans and shaft of the penis (frenulum), eliminating multiple choice D. The patient is not having the circumcision for the first time, but needed a repair from a previous circumcision, eliminating multiple choice answers A and B.

16. D. 56441

The key term to narrow your choices down is the removal of "labial adhesions". This is found in the code descriptive for multiple choice answer D, 56441.

17. C. 62365, 62355-51, T85.79XA

This was a removal of an intrathecal catheter and pump, eliminating multiple choice answer D. The pump is not being implanted or replaced eliminating multiple choice answer B. Nor is the intrathecal catheter being implanted, revised or repositioned eliminating multiple choice answer A.

Diagnosis Rationale: This was a surgical complication; an infection due to an implant, eliminating multiple choice answers A and D.

18. B. 62223

This key word to choose the correct shunt being performed is "ventriculo-peritoneal", leading you to multiple choice answer B.

19. C. 64721

The key term to choose the correct answer is "median nerve", found in code 64721.

20. D. 67808

There is more than a single chalazion to be removed, eliminating multiple choice answer C. The chalazion was on the upper and lower lid, eliminating multiple choice answer A. The patient was under general anesthesia, eliminating multiple choice answer B.

21. B. 99211, Z46.89

Scenario documents patient returning to the gynecologist guiding you to the codes for established patient office visit. This eliminates multiple choices A and C. For this scenario, the patient did not have any complaints that required the presence of a physician. There was no examination or medical making decision performed for the patient guiding you to code 99211. There must be an order for the patient to come in for the office visit. For the diagnosis code, the pessary was removed for cleaning reporting Z46.89 Encounter for fitting and adjustment of other specified devices. (Refer to ICD-10-CM guideline I.A.9)

22. C. 99221

   According to CPT® guidelines: When the patient is admitted to the hospital as an inpatient in the course of an encounter in another site of service (example, hospital emergency department, observation status in a hospital, physician's office, nursing facility) all evaluation and management services provided by that physician in conjunction with that admission are considered part of the initial hospital care when performed on the same date of service.

   Meaning for this scenario the patient's physician had come to the ER and also admitted the patient on the same date of service, eliminating multiple choices A and B.

   All three of the key components of an initial hospital care code must be met or exceeded. 99221 requires: detailed or comprehensive history, detailed or comprehensive examination, and straightforward or low complexity medical decision making. Because the lowest key component in the question is a detailed history, the highest level that can be reached is 99221. To report code 99222 you would need a comprehensive history.

23. A. 99468-25, 93303-26

According to CPT® subsection guidelines under Inpatient Neonatal and Pediatric Critical Care: If the same physician provides critical care services for a neonatal or pediatric patient in both the outpatient and inpatient setting on the same day, report only the appropriate Neonatal or Pediatric Critical Care codes 99468-99476 for all critical care services provided on that day. This eliminates multiple choice answers C and D. The baby is 20 days-old and you cannot bill intubation (31500) and ventilation management with the neonatal and pediatric critical care codes, eliminating multiple choice B.

24. C. 00862-P2, C65.9, E11.9

The patient receives anesthesia for a laparoscopic radical nephrectomy. Look the CPT® Index, for Anesthesia/Nephrectomy. You are referred to 00862. Review the code in the numeric section to verify accuracy. The patient has controlled type 2 diabetes which supports the use of P2. The patient has renal pelvis cancer. The distinction of secondary cancer is not made so the cancer is coded as a primary neoplasm. Go to the Table of Neoplasms and look for Neoplasm, neoplastic/kidney/pelvis/Malignant Primary column. You are referred to C65.-. Complete code in the Tabular List, C65.9. The patient also has controlled type 2 diabetes. Look in the ICD-10-CM Alphabetic Index for Diabetes/type 2 referring you to E11.9.

25. C. 01830-QS-P1

The patient receives monitored anesthesia care also known as MAC which is reported with HCPCS Level II modifier QS. There is no indication the patient has a history of cardiopulmonary condition so G9 would not be appropriate. Look in the CPT® Index for Anesthesia/Forearm. You are referred to multiple codes (00400, 01810-01820, 01830-01860). Refer to these codes in the numeric section to determine the correct code using the code descriptions. The procedure was open and performed on the distal radius. The appropriate code is 01830.

26. B. 00326

The patient receives general anesthesia for the removal of a laryngeal mass. Look in the CPT® Index for Anesthesia/Larynx. You are referred to 00320 and 00326. Review the code descriptions in the numeric section. Code 00326 is the correct code to indicate the procedure is performed on a patient younger than one year. 99100 is not reported because the patient's age range is included in the description of the anesthesia code. There is a parenthetical note under 00326 that indicates the code should not be reported with 99100.

27. D. 36247, 75710-26

Selecting the correct answer can be tackled two ways:

(1) A third order selective catheter placement in the brachiocephalic system was not performed, eliminating multiple choice answers A and C. Bilateral angiography of the lower extremities was not performed, eliminating multiple choice answer B. Arterial access was the left common femoral artery and the catheter was directed into the right common iliac (36245 - first order) into right external iliac (36246-second order). The catheter was then directed to the common femoral into the superficial femoral artery (36247-third order). Report only the highest level of catheter placement 36247. Angiography for the right extremity is 75710. Modifier 26 denotes the professional service.

OR

(2) A right lower extremity angiogram was performed. Code 75736 is eliminated because that is for the pelvis. Code 75716 is eliminated because that is if both extremities had an

angiogram. Code 75658 is eliminated because that is for the brachial artery. Code 75710 is the correct angiography code.

28. C. 77067

The radiological service is a screening mammogram of both breasts eliminating multiple choices A, B and D. Note: If this was a bilateral diagnostic mammogram you only report code 77066 because the code is specifically for both breasts. You will not report 77065 and 77066, or report 77065 twice or with a modifier 50. Code 77066 also does not have modifier 50 appended because the code description already indicates that it is a bilateral code.

29. B. 52332-50, 74420-26

This procedure was performed bilaterally (stents placed in the right and left ureter), eliminating multiple choice answer A and C. The pyelogram was retrograde, eliminating multiple choice answer D. Retrograde pyelogram is included in cystoscopy, 52005. The stent placement 52332-50 correctly reports the bilateral procedure. Modifier 26 is correctly appended to 74420 because the procedure was performed in an outpatient facility with the physician interpreting the radiological service.

30. **B. 88305-26, 88304-26**

    Code 88305 - Skin, other than cyst/tag/debridement/plastic repair is for the cutaneous ulceration on the left leg. Code 88304 - Artery, atheromatous plaque is for the arterial plaque taken from the femoral artery. Modifier 26 is appended to show the pathologist's service.

31. **B. 88331-26, 88307-26**

    The pathology consultation of the tumor is performed during a surgery guiding you to code 88331. Code 88331 is only reported once because one block is submitted. Codes 80500 and 80502 are reported according to CPT® guidelines when the pathologist gives a response to a request from an attending physician in relation to a test result(s) requiring additional medical interpretive judgment. A gross and microscopic examination was also performed reporting code 88307.

32. D. 80053, 8233

Subsection guidelines in the CPT® codebook under Organ or Disease-Oriented Panels state: "Do not report two or more panel codes that include any of the same constituent tests performed from the same patient collection. If a group of tests overlaps two or more panels, report the panel that incorporates the greater number of tests to fulfill the code definition and report the remaining tests using individual test codes." The comprehensive metabolic panel has the greater number of tests than the basic metabolic panel, eliminating multiple choice answers A and C. Code 82330 (Calcium, ionized) is not listed under panel code 80053, and because that is the remaining test in the basic metabolic panel that is not included in the comprehensive metabolic panel it is also reported, eliminating multiple choice answer B.

33. C. 90713, 90660, 90716, 90471, 90472, 90474

The young child was administered the Poliovirus vaccine by intramuscular route guiding you to code 90713. The influenza vaccine was for intranasal route is code 90660 eliminating multiple choices A and D. For the administration codes the vaccines were administered without face-to-face counseling eliminating multiple choice answer B. The first vaccination was administered by the intramuscular route guiding you to code 90471. The second vaccine (additional vaccine) was administered by the intranasal route guiding you to code 90474. The third vaccine (additional vaccine) is given by the subcutaneous route guiding you to code 90472.

34. D. 90945

Patient is having an evaluation for peritoneal dialysis eliminating multiple choices A and B. There is no documentation in the scenario where the physician repeated the dialysis evaluation of the patient due to a complication, eliminating multiple choice C.

35. A. 92014-25, 92071-5

Patient is having an ophthalmological evaluation service provided, eliminating multiple choice B. The contact lens is being fitted for a therapeutic use, eliminating multiple choice answers C and D.

36. C. 92520-52

The patient is having a laryngeal function study in which an acoustic test was performed, eliminating multiple choice answer B. The test is not performed with an endoscope, eliminating multiple choice D. The aerodynamic testing was not performed on this visit so modifier 52 is appended due to a parenthetical note that indicates: For performance of a single test, use modifier 52.

37. A. Entropion is the inward turning of the eyelid and ectropion is the outward turning of the eyelid.

Multiple choice A is the correct answer. In the ICD-10-CM Alphabetic Index look for Entropion (eyelid), H02.009. Ectropion is H02.109. In the Tabular List category H02 is for other disorders of the eyelid.

38. A. Anesthesia for intraperitoneal procedures in lower abdomen including laparoscopy; radical hysterectomy

Code 00846 is an indented code, which means the description from code 00840 up to the semicolon is the beginning of the full description for code 00846. Multiple choice A is the correct answer for the full code description.

39. B. Hernias

These are types of hernias. CPT® codes 49491-49657 are categorized by the type of hernias to be repaired.

40. C. Pelvis

The acetabulum is the cup-shaped socket of the hip joint which is part of the pelvis. You can locate this answer in the ICD-10-CM codebook. In the ICD-10-CM Alphabetic Index look for Fracture, traumatic/pelvis and you will see acetabulum listed under pelvis.

41. A. Foot

The abductor hallucis is a muscle of the foot that abducts the big toe. In the CPT® Index look for Tenotomy. There are many anatomical areas to choose from, but you will find this muscle located in the description of code 28240. All the codes in that section deal with the foot.

42. C. R87.619, Z85.41

According to ICD-10-CM guidelines (Section I.C.2.d): When a primary malignancy has been previously excised or eradicated from its site and there is no further treatment directed to that site and there is no evidence of any existing primary malignancy, a code from category Z85,

Personal history of malignant neoplasm, should be used to indicate the former site of the malignancy. The scenario indicates the patient had a history of cervical cancer, and for two years had Pap smears performed to check for the cancer not returning meaning the patient does not have current adenocarcinoma of the cervix. This eliminates multiple choice answers A and B. The reason she is going into surgery is due to a last cervix Pap smear coming back with abnormal results, eliminating multiple choice answer D.

43. C. J18.9

According to ICD-10-CM guidelines (Section I.B.4): Codes that describe symptoms and signs, as opposed to diagnoses, are acceptable for reporting purposes when a related definitive diagnosis has not been established (confirmed) by the provider. For this scenario a definitive diagnosis was confirmed by the physician with the patient having pneumonia, eliminating multiple choice answers A and B. The diagnosis is double pneumonia. Look in the ICD-10-CM

Alphabetic Index for Pneumonia. The term "double" is found in parenthesis next to the main term Pneumonia. According to ICD-10-CM Coding Guidelines, I.A.7.: ( ) Parentheses are used in both the Alphabetic Index and Tabular List to enclose supplementary words that may be present or absent in the statement of a disease or procedure without affecting the code number to which it is assigned. The terms within the parentheses are referred to as nonessential modifiers. That means because the word double is in parentheses next to Pneumonia it is a supplementary word used for diagnosing the disease and if it is documented with pneumonia you report code J18.9 for that diagnosis, eliminating multiple choice D.

44. C. R00.1, T40.2X5A

The Demerol was not taken as an accidental overdose, wrong substance given or taken, an assault, nor for self-harm, eliminating multiple choices A, B and D. It is an adverse effect to a drug that has been correctly prescribed or properly administered. According to ICD-10-CM guidelines (Section I.C.19.e.5): Code first the nature of the adverse effect followed by the appropriate code for the adverse effect of the drug (T36-T50). Bradycardia (R00.1) is reported first then adverse effect to Demerol (T40.2X5A).

45. B. These codes have sequencing priority over codes from other chapters.
     According to ICD-10-CM guidelines (Section I.C.15.a.1): Chapter 15 codes have sequencing priority over codes from other chapters. Additional codes from other chapters may be used in conjunction with chapter 15 codes to further specify conditions.

46. C. G0120
    Patient is not having a flexible sigmoidoscopy performed for the colorectal cancer screening, eliminating multiple choice A. The screening for the cancer is being performed via barium enema instead of a colonoscopy. This eliminates multiple choices B and D. This patient is qualified by Medicare to be a high risk by having

a history of ulcerative colitis. An individual with ulcerative enteritis or a history of a malignant neoplasm of the lower gastrointestinal tract is considered at high-risk for colorectal cancer, as defined by CMS.

47. C. Protected health information

    Protected health information under the Health Information Portability and Accountability Act (HIPAA) is any information, whether oral or recorded, in any form or medium that is created or received by a health care provider, health plan, public health authority, employer, life insurer, school or university, or health care clearinghouse relating to the past, present, or future physical or mental health or condition of an individual, the provision of health services to that individual, or payment around those services. Only health information at the individual level is covered; health information of groups is not.

48. C. Returning to the operating room the next day for a complication resulting from the initial procedure

    The CPT® surgical package definition is in the Surgery Guidelines found in the CPT® codebook (right after the Anesthesia section of codes). Multiple choice C is the correct answer, because modifier 78 is reported on a procedure code to indicate a patient's return to the OR for a complication (unplanned return) that has occurred during the postoperative period of the initial procedure.

49. A. If the type of diabetes mellitus is not documented in the medical record the default type is E11.- Type 2 diabetes mellitus

    The ICD-10-CM coding guidelines for diabetes mellitus are found in Section I.C.4. Multiple choice A is the correct answer, this guideline is in Section I.C.4.a.2.

50. D. External cause codes should never be sequenced as a first-listed or primary code

Multiple choice D is the correct answer. The ICD-10-CM guidelines for the External Causes Of Morbidity (V00-Y99) is in Section I.C.20.

51. A. 19081

To start narrowing your choices was the biopsy performed percutaneously or by an open incision? The operative note documents that a "SenoRx needle" was used to obtain the biopsy, which is percutaneous. Because there was a biopsy and a placement of a localization device (clip), you eliminate multiple choice B. Code 19283 is reported only for the placement of the localization device. Stereotactic image was used to perform the needle biopsy and placement of the clip. This eliminates multiple choice D, because code 19100 is for needle biopsy without imaging guidance. Code 19081 is the only code reported for the operative note because its code description reports both the biopsy and the placement of the clip under stereotactic imaging, eliminating multiple choice C.

52. B. 11310, 11100-59

The first procedure performed was the lesion on the lower lip removed by the shaving technique. Reported with code 11310. The punch biopsy is performed on the lesion located on the nose. Reported with code 11100. Modifier 59 indicates that the biopsy was totally separate performed on another lesion, otherwise it is bundled with 11310.

53. C. 15822-50

Patient is having a blepharoplasty done on the upper eyelids, eliminating multiple choice answer D. There is no indication in the scenario that excessive skin weighing down the lid had to be excised, eliminating multiple choice answers A and B. Modifier 50 is appended to indicate the procedure was performed on both eyelids.

54. D. 29825-LT

To narrow down your choices decide if the procedure is an open procedure or performed with an arthroscope? It was performed with an arthroscope, eliminating multiple choice answers A and B. The diagnostic arthroscopy (29805) is a separate procedure, and according to CPT® Surgery Guidelines: The codes designated as "separate procedure" should not be reported in addition to the code for the total procedure or service of which it is considered an integral component. Meaning code 29806 already includes the diagnostic arthroscopy code, so you only report code 29806. Code 29806 represents suturing of the capsule (capsulorrhaphy); however, this was not the procedure performed. The procedure performed was a lysis of adhesions for a frozen shoulder (29825) noted in multiple choice answer D.

55. A. 22612, 22614 x 2, 22842, 20938, 20930

To start narrowing the correct arthrodesis code to report, you first need to determine the surgical approach. The scenario tells us that the patient was placed in prone position (lying face down) on the table and a lumbar incision was made indicating a posterior approach, eliminating multiple choices B and D. The next bit of information to look for is the technique that was used for the arthrodesis, which was the interbody fusion technique guiding you to code 22630.

56. B. 25605- LT, 20690-51

In the body of the note after the Procedure heading it states, "the fracture was manipulated", eliminating multiple choice answer A. Was the fracture treatment opened or closed? There is no indication in the operative note that the patient was surgically opened at the fracture site to treat it, eliminating multiple choice answer D. The key words to choose the correct code between B and C are external fixation system and external fixator; where pins are connected to bone and to an external fixator to help the fracture heal. The fixator was a uniplane system as only one external fixator was applied in one plane (20690).

57. A. 33208

The patient is having an insertion of a pace maker, eliminating multiple choice answers C and D. A subcutaneous pocket was created for the pacemaker generator and the leads connected to the generator were placed in the atrium and ventricle leading you to multiple choice answer A. Fluoroscopy is included and should not be reported separately.

58. C. 32670

The removal of the lobes are performed thorascopically not by an open approach, eliminating multiple choices A and B. The entire right lung is not removed, only two lobes (upper and middle) in the right lung are removed, eliminating multiple choice D.

59. D. 32552-58

You can start narrowing your choices by the modifiers. Appendix A in the CPT® codebook lists the numeric modifiers. The key phrase to choose the correct modifier is "planned return", which is found in the descriptive for modifier 58. The patient is returning to surgery to remove the pleural catheter, eliminating multiple choice B.

60. D. 33641, Q21.1

The patient had an atrial septal defect, eliminating multiple choice answers A and C. The surgery was only performed on the atrial septum, eliminating multiple choice answer B. According to ICD-10-CM Coding Guidelines (Section I.B.5): Signs and symptoms that are associated routinely with a disease process should not be assigned as additional codes, unless otherwise instructed by the classification. Shortness of breath (R06.02) is a symptom of an atrial septum defect and would not be coded.

61. C. 44005-22

This surgical procedure was not performed by a laparoscope, it was an open surgery, eliminating multiple choice answers B and D. It is documented that the adhesions were "extensive," "time consuming," and "spending an extra hour" to free up the attachments to the gastrointestinal tract. These are key words in indicating modifier 22 should be appended to the procedure code. Appendix A lists the modifiers.

62. **B. 43241-52**

An esophagogastroduodenoscopy (also known as an upper GI endoscopy or EGD) is performed, not an esophagoscopy which is only an inspection of the esophagus, eliminating multiple choice D. The EGD was performed along with a placement of a catheter, eliminating multiple choice answer C. Since the placement was a catheter, multiple choice answer A is eliminated. The correct answer is 43241 with modifier -52 appended to indicate that the endoscope did not pass into the duodenum. According to CPT® guidelines, if a reason is given why the duodenum was not examined and a repeat examination is not planned, append modifier 52 to the EGD codes.

63. A. 44120-78

The surgery was not performed with a laparoscope, eliminating multiple choice answer D. The patient did not have a diagnosis of congenital atresia, eliminating multiple choice answer B. This was an unplanned return to the operating room due to the patient having a complication from the original surgery that was performed a week ago, eliminating multiple choice answer C.

64. B. 44143

The surgery was not performed by a laparoscope, eliminating multiple choice answer D. The patient had a colostomy (Artificial surgical opening anywhere along the length of the colon to the skin surface for the diversion of feces) done, not an anastomosis (surgically creating a connection between bowel segments to allow flow from one to the other), eliminating multiple choice answer A. The operative note documents that the distal left colon was divided and the sigmoid colon excised, eliminating multiple choice answer C.

65. A. 54304

Patient does not have a penile injury, eliminating multiple choice D. The patient is not having an insertion of a penile prosthesis, eliminating multiple choice C. The surgery is not correcting a hypospadias complication such as a fistula, stricture, or diverticula, eliminating multiple choice answer B. The correct answer is A, 54304.

66. B. 59841

Patient is terminating her pregnancy by dilation and evacuation (D&E), eliminating multiple choice answer A. There is no documentation of this being an incomplete abortion, eliminating multiple choice answer C. The abortion was not induced by intra-amniotic injection(s), eliminating multiple choice answer D.

67. B. 58661, 58563-51

One way to narrow down the choices is to code for the endometrial ablation using the hysteroscope. Because the endometrial ablation was done with hysteroscopic guidance, multiple choice answer A is eliminated. No biopsies were taken or polyps removed eliminating multiple choice answer C. The removal of her ovaries and fallopian tubes (oophorectomy and salpingectomy) were performed by a laparoscope, eliminating multiple choice answer D.

68. D. 63045, 63048 x 2

Laminectomy was performed, eliminating multiple choice answer B. Facetectomy and foraminotomy were performed, eliminating multiple choice answer C. The laminectomy is performed bilaterally on three segments of the cervical. Modifier 50 is not appended to code 63045-63048, because the code descriptive has a parenthetical note indicating that these codes

include unilateral or bilateral, eliminating
multiple answer A.

69. C. 66982

The surgery is an extracapsular cataract
removal, eliminating multiple choice D. The
removal of the cataract and the insertion of the
lens were performed at the same time,
eliminating multiple choice A. The keyword to
choose between codes 66982 and 66984 is "iris
expansion device" which was used to remove
the cataract, eliminating multiple choice answer
B.

70. A. 69436-50, H65.33

The patient is under general anesthesia
eliminating multiple choice answer C. A
ventilating tube was placed in the ears
eliminating multiple choice answer D. Look in
the ICD-10-CM Alphabetic Index for
Otitis/media/non-suppurative/chronic/mucoid,
mucous guiding you to code H65.3-. Go to the

Tabular List to complete code, H65.33.

Eliminating multiple choice answer B.

71. A. 99215

E/M Guidelines: "When counseling and/or
coordination of care dominates (more than 50%)
the physician/patient and/or family encounter
(face-to-face in the office or other outpatient
setting or floor/unit time in the hospital or
nursing facility), then time may be considered
the key or controlling factor to qualify for a
particular level of E/M services." E/M level 99215
is the correct code to report, because it has in
its code description, "Typically, 40 minutes are
spent face-to-face with the patient and/or
family." In the question there is a total time
given of 40 minutes spent face-to-face with the
patient, in which more than half of that time (25
minutes) was on counseling the patient.

72. C. 99233

The scenario indicates to select an evaluation and management service for the physician evaluating the patient on the following day of admission, eliminating multiple choice B; code 99221 is reported for when the patient is initially admitted to the hospital. The patient is not in observation status in which the patient was admitted and discharged on the same date of service, eliminating multiple choice answer D. There is no request documented in the scenario for another physician to recommend care for the condition, eliminating multiple choice A. Subsequent hospital care codes require meeting or exceeding two of three key components. Code 99233 is correct because a detailed and detailed exam are the two key components that meet.

73. B. 99219

According to CPT® subsection guidelines under Initial Observation Care: When "observation status" is initiated in the course of an encounter in another site of service (example, hospital emergency department, physician's office, nursing facility) all evaluation and management services provided by the supervising physician in conjunction with initiating "observation status" are considered part of the initial observation care when performed on the same date. Meaning you will not report an emergency service code since the patient was placed in observation care from the ER on the same date of service, eliminating multiple choice C. CPT® subsection guidelines add: Evaluation and management services on the same date provided in sites that are related to initiating "observation status" should not be reported separately. This eliminates multiple choice A. Patient was not admitted and discharged in observation status on the same date of service, eliminating multiple choice D.

74. C. 00172, 99100

The patient receives general anesthesia for the repair of a cleft palate. Look in the CPT® Index, for Anesthesia/Cleft Palate Repair referring you to 00172. Verify the code description in the

numeric section for accuracy. The patient is 6
months old, 99100 is appropriate for this
scenario.

75. B. 00402

The patient had a previous mastectomy. For this
encounter the mastopexy and reconstruction is
performed. Look in the CPT® Index, for
Anesthesia/Breast referring you to 00402-00406.
Refer to the code descriptions in the numeric
section. 00402 is the correct code for anesthesia
administered for breast reconstruction.

76. C. 01402-AA, 62326, 01996 x 2

A code is selected for the general anesthesia
performed for the total knee replacement. Look
in the CPT® Index, for
Anesthesia/Replacement/Knee. You are referred
to 01402. The continuous lumbar epidural
infusion is also reported because the purpose is
for postoperative pain. There is no indication
that imaging guidance was used. The procedure
is reported with 62326. There is a parenthetical

note following 62327 that indicates to use 01996 in conjunction with 62324-62327. 01996 is a per day code. In this scenario, the physician performs two days of daily management. Modifier AA indicates the anesthesia was performed by an anesthesiologist.

77. C. 71020

Only two chest X-ray views were taken (AP and lateral), eliminating multiple choices B and D. The chest X-rays were taken in the physician's office and interpreted so there are no modifiers appended to the code. If the chest X-ray was performed somewhere else (for example, outpatient facility) and the films were sent to the physician for his interpretation then modifier 26 would be appended to the code.

78. D. 55875, 76965-26

Radioactive seeds were inserted directly into the prostate transperineally using needles (percutaneous), in selecting code 55875.

79. A. 73100-26, S52.502B, W18.31XA, Y92.039

The X-ray was taken in two views (oblique and lateral) without arthrography, eliminating multiple choice answers B and C. The fracture is an open fracture. Look in the ICD-10-CM Alphabetic Index for Fracture, traumatic/radius/lower end referring you to S52.50-. Turn to the Tabular List to complete the code, S52.502B.

80. B. 80305, 80338

To report codes for drug testing depends on the method of the testing. The scenario indicates a chemistry analyzer utilizing immunoassay method was used, guiding you to code 80307. Subsection guidelines for Presumptive Drug Class Screening indicates: Use 80307 once to report single or multiple procedures, classes, or results on any date of service. A drug confirmation was performed on antidepressants, reporting code 80338 because the type of antidepressant is not documented.

81. C. 80201

The lab test being performed in this scenario is for therapeutic drug monitoring to assist the physician in drug regimen adjustment to reach an optimal drug concentration ensuring an adequate therapeutic response without drug-induced adverse effects, guiding you to codes 80150-80299. The patient is not having a drug screening test in which the physician is determining a specific drug present or not present in the patient (qualitative) eliminating multiple choice answers A and D. Therapeutic Drug Assay codes are performed to monitor clinical response to a known, prescribed medication.

82. D. 82951, 82952 x 2

The test being performed is a glucose tolerance test (GTT) guiding you to code 82951. Five blood specimens were taken in which the first three blood specimens are reported with code 82951. The last two blood specimens will be reported with code 82952 twice.

83. B. 82810, 82810-91

The physician requests a blood gas for oxygen saturation (O_2) only, guiding you to code 82810. Modifier 51 is appended to surgical procedure codes meaning because this code is a lab code, modifier 51 is inappropriate, eliminating multiple choice answers A and C. There is no mention of an outside lab, eliminating multiple choice D. The physician would also report 36600 for the arterial puncture.

84. D. 93018-26, 99204-25

All three components are documented to report code 93015, in which the cardiologist is supervising, he owns the equipment (tracing), because the test is being performed in the office, and the physician interpreted the test. Modifier 26 would be inappropriate to append to code 93015, it denotes the global service.

85. A. 96360

   Patient is having a hydration infusion
   eliminating multiple choices C and D. The add-
   on-code is incorrect to report for this scenario. A
   parenthetical statement states: (Report 96361
   for hydration infusion intervals of greater than
   30 beyond 1 hour increments) meaning if the
   hydration infusion is 30 minutes or less you
   would not report 96361.

86. A. 97168, Z51.89, G35

   This patient is coming in for occupational
   therapy which helps a patient to improve basic
   motor functions and reasoning abilities for
   independent daily living. This eliminates
   multiple choices B and D. This is a re-evaluation
   visit eliminating multiple choice C. The first
   listed diagnosis code is Z51.89 because the
   patient is receiving after care for occupational
   therapy.

87. D. Osteomyelitis

Osteomyelitis is an inflammation of bone and bone marrow caused by a bacterial infection which can lead to a reduction of blood supply to the bone. In the ICD-10-CM Alphabetical Index look for Inflammation/bone-see Osteomyelitis.

88. A. Hair

Trich/o means hair. In the ICD-10-CM Alphabetical Index look for a diagnosis that starts with Trich. Trichorrhexis refers you to code L67.0. In the Tabular List category code L67 is for Hair color and hair shaft abnormalities.

89. B. Occipital lobe

The series of terms are lobes found in the brain. You can find an illustration of the brain showing the different lobes in your CPT® codebook in the beginning of the Nervous System section.

90. D. Surgical reconstruction of the renal pelvis

Pyeloplasty is the surgical reconstruction or revision of the pelvis of the kidney (renal) to correct an obstruction. The CPT® Index refers you to codes 50400-50405, and 50544 for Pyeloplasty. The code is found under the Repair heading in the numeric section and the code description states "plastic operation on renal pelvis" to help you know what is being performed.

91. C. T23.301A, T23.302A, T20.20XA, T31.10, X10.2XXA, Y93.G

The burn was not caused by a chemical, eliminating multiple choice D. According to ICD-10-CM guidelines (Section I.C.19.d.1): Sequence first the code that reflects the highest degree of burn when more than one burn is present. This eliminates multiple choice A. When reporting the percentage of body burns (T31.-) you first need to know the total percentage of the body burned. For our scenario the total percentage of the body burned is 10 percent (5% face + 5%

hands = 10%) T31.1-. The hands had 5 percent third degree burn guiding you T31.10.

92. C. K74.60, I85.11

    In the ICD-10-CM Alphabetic Index look for Varix/esophagus/in/cirrhosis of liver/bleeding referring you to code I85.11. This eliminates multiple choices A and D. In the Tabular List you will see an instructional note above codes I85.10 and I85.11 to Code first underlying disease. Meaning for the scenario cirrhosis of liver (K47.60) is coded first then the esophageal varices with bleeding is coded as a secondary code. Eliminating multiple choice B.

93. D. R26.0, S82.002S

    According to ICD-10-CM guidelines (Section I.B.10): A sequela is the residual effect (condition produced) after the acute phase of an illness or injury has terminated. There is no time limit on when a sequela code can be used. The code for the acute phase of an illness or injury that led to the sequela is never used with a code for the late effect. This eliminates multiple choice answers A and B. The guidelines further state: Coding of late effects generally requires two codes sequenced in the following order: The condition or nature of the sequela is sequenced first. The sequela code is sequenced second. This eliminates multiple choice C.

94. C. Z codes may be used either as a primary code or a secondary code.

According to ICD-10-CM Coding Guidelines (Section I.C.21.a): Z codes are for use in any healthcare setting. Z codes may be used as either a first-listed (principal diagnosis code in the inpatient setting) or secondary code, depending on the circumstances of the encounter. Certain Z codes may only be used as first-listed, others only as secondary codes. Multiple Choice C is the correct answer.

95. B. V2785

The key word to guide you to HCPCS code V2785 is cornea. The scenario addresses the code description. The donor cornea preparation indicates the processing, then the donor cornea being stored indicates the preserving and it being rinsed and transferred indicates the transporting.

96. A. J3301 x 4

The injection given is Kenalog-10 eliminating multiple choices C and D. 40 mg of the Kenalog-10 was given. Code J3301 is reported for 10 mg so it will have to be reported four times to cover 40 mg.

97. A. A digital X-ray

While B, C, or D might be done electronically, by definition they aren't required to be done electronically. A digital X-ray is an X-ray with an image that is stored electronically rather than on film, and so A is the correct answer.

98. C. Workers' compensation

Workers' compensation is excluded from the definition of a health plan under the Health Insurance Portability and Accountability Act (HIPAA). Therefore, Workers' compensation plans are not required to meet HIPAA standards for privacy, security or code sets.

99. B. ICD-10-CM

ICD-10-CM guidelines are the only guidelines specifically mentioned in HIPAA. While HIPAA requires the use of the other code sets listed, there is no specific mention of the other guidelines in the law. This information is found in the ICD-10-CM Official Guidelines for Coding and Reported in you ICD-10-CM codebook: These guidelines are a set of rules that have been developed to accompany and complement the official conventions and instructions provided within the ICD-10-CM itself. These guidelines are based on the coding and sequencing instructions in Volumes I, II and III of ICD-10-CM, but provide additional instruction. Adherence to these guidelines when assigning

ICD-10-CM diagnosis and procedure codes is required under the Health Insurance Portability and Accountability Act (HIPAA).

100. A. If the patient has an underdose of insulin due to an insulin pump malfunction.

The ICD-10-CM guidelines (Section I.C.4.a.5): An underdose of insulin due to an insulin pump failure should be assigned T85.6-, as the principal or first listed code, followed by code T83.3X6-. Additional codes for the type of diabetes mellitus should also be assigned.

101. D. 17313,17314, 17315

Patient is having Mohs Micrographic Surgery being performed only, eliminating multiple choice answer C. Mohs codes are based on the anatomic grouping by code, the number of stages taken, and number of blocks per stage. The surgery was on the back reporting code 17313 for stage 1 with three blocks, add-on code 17314 is for stage 2 with five blocks, and add-on code 17315 is for the sixth block in stage 2.

102.   A. 14060

An adjacent tissue transfer (advancement flap) was used to repair a defect on the nose due to an excision of a malignant lesion, eliminating multiple choice answers C and D. The section guidelines in the CPT® codebook for Adjacent Tissue or Rearrangement indicate that the excision of a benign lesion (11400-11446) or a malignant lesion (11600-11646) is included in codes for adjacent tissue transfer (14000-14302), and are not separately reported. This eliminates multiple choice answer B.

103.   C. 11004

The abscess had already burst, with no need to perform an incision to open it, eliminating multiple choice answers A and B. The difference between multiple choice answers C and D, is that the patient is having the debridement performed due to a soft tissue infection in the perineum area. The correct code is 11004 for debridement of necrotized infected tissue on the external genitalia.

104.   D. 19125, D24.2

You can narrow your choices down by the diagnosis. The beginning of the operative note documents that core biopsies showed "papilloma". In the ICD-10-CM Alphabetic Index, look for Papilloma-see also Neoplasm, benign, by site. Go to the Table of Neoplasms and look for Neoplasm, neoplastic/breast/Benign (column) refers you to code D24.-. Turn to the Tabular List to complete the code, D24.2. Procedure code 19125 is correct because preoperative placement of radiologic marker (preoperative needle localization with hookwire needle injection with methylene blue) was used to excise the lesion.

105.   A. 26123-RT, 26125-F7

The patient is having a fasciectomy, eliminating multiple choice answers C and D. The fasciectomy was performed on the right hand supported by the documentation that states: "the fascial attachments to the flexor tendon sheath were released" and "subtotal palmar fasciectomy." Documentation also indicates the right middle finger (modifier F7) had diseased fascia excised.

106.   C. 27096-50

The injection is being performed in the sacroiliac joint, eliminating multiple choice answer A. Fluoroscopic guidance is included and should not be reported separately because the code description for code 27096 includes imaging, eliminating multiple choice answers B and D. There is parenthetical note under code 27096 that indicates to use modifier 50 for bilateral procedure (left and right).

107.   C. 29881-RT, M23.221, M65.861, M94.261, M22.41

For this operative note the anatomic location is the knee, specifically with just the medial meniscus performed on, eliminating multiple choice answers A and D. A limited synovectomy (29875) was performed; however, it was performed in the medial compartment of the knee along with the medial meniscectomy;

therefore, is not reported. Also, code 29875 is a separate procedure, according to CPT® Surgery Guidelines: The codes designated as "separate procedure" should not be reported in addition to the code for the total procedure or service of which it is considered an integral component. Debridement was performed in the lateral and patellofemoral compartments which is included in code 29881; code 29877 is not reported separately.

Synovitis (M65.861), chondromalacia (M94.261) for the fibrillated articular cartilage of the tibial plateau and patella (M22.41) are reported. The patient had a meniscus tear, but the operative note indicates a more specific area of the tear. It documents that, "An upbiting basket was introduced to transect the base of the posterior horn flap tear", look in the ICD-10-CM Alphabetic Index for Tear/meniscus/old-see Derangement, knee, meniscus due to old tear. Look for Derangement/knee/meniscus/medial/posterior horn M23.22-. Go to the Tabular List to complete the code, M23.221.

108.   D. 22318

The procedure performed is the reduction of an odontoid fracture, by incising (open treatment) the anterior neck (anterior approach) to reduce the fracture and placement of internal fixation (Kirschner wire and lag screw). Gardner-Wells tongs (20660) were applied originally to try to reduce the fracture with axial traction; however, this procedure is listed as a separate procedure and it should not be reported during the same session for reduction of the fracture.

109.   C. 36831-78

Modifier needs to be appended to procedure code 36831 because the patient returned to surgery within the postoperative period, eliminating multiple choice answer B. Appendix A lists the modifiers needed to append to the procedure codes. The patient did not have a planned return to surgery, eliminating multiple choice answer D. Nor did the patient have a repeat procedure on the same day of service, eliminating multiple choice answer A. The patient had to return to the operating room to have a thrombectomy and balloon angioplasty of the venous anastomosis due to the AV graft failing which is a complication that followed the initial procedure. Modifier 78 indicates is correct.

110.   A. 37609

The key terms for this scenario are "temporal artery biopsy", which is found in the code description for multiple choice answer A.

111.   C. 38505, 76942-26

A needle was used to obtain the biopsies, eliminating multiple choice answers B and D. An aspiration (drawing fluid out) was not performed, eliminating multiple choice answer A. There is a parenthetical note under code 38505 that indicates see imaging guidance, when performed 76942, 77012, 77021. Imaging guidance (ultrasound) was performed, correctly reporting 76942.

112.   B. 44960, 49905, K35.3

Patient had an open surgery appendectomy,
eliminating multiple choice answer D. The
scenario documents that there was also an
abscess, eliminating A and C. 44905 is an add-on
code, which modifier 51 is not reported. Look in
the ICD-10-CM Alphabetic Index for
Appendicitis/with peritoneal abscess, referring
you to code K35.3. Verify code in the Tabular
List.

113.   C. 42826, 42106-51

The selection of your code is based on the age of
the patient and what was excised. The age of
this patient is 15, eliminating multiple choice
answer B. The patient only had tonsils removed
eliminating multiple choice A. Part of the uvula
was also removed, eliminating multiple choice
answer D.

114.   D. 49560, 49568

The selection of the hernia repair codes are
based on the type of hernia, surgical approach

(open vs laparoscopy), and complication factor if it is reduced vs incarcerated or strangulated. Some hernia codes are based on age. The surgery was not performed by a laparoscope, eliminating multiple choice answer C. There is no mention of the hernia being incarcerated or strangulated, eliminating multiple choice answer B. According to CPT® guidelines in the hernia repair section, codes 49560-49566 can be reported with mesh add-on code, 49568. You will also see a parenthetical under add-on code 49568 that also indicates what codes can be reported with it.

115.   D. 59120

Procedure had started with a laparoscopic treatment for a tubal ectopic pregnancy. Due to the patient's body size the laparoscopic approach was terminated and an open surgery was performed instead, eliminating multiple choice answers A and B. The patient had the left fallopian tube removed (salpingectomy) removed, eliminating multiple choice answer C. When a laparoscopic surgical procedure fails, only the successful open procedure is reported (NCCI Manual, version 6.1, April-June, 2000).

116.   C. 59514, O82, Z37.0, Z3A.39

The selection of the CPT® delivery codes listed are based on the global information of the patient's history care. The documentation does not have information on the history of either the pregnancy care or previous pregnancies so a global code cannot be coded. There is no documentation that supports the patient had a previous cesarean, eliminating multiple choice answer A. There is no documentation that supports patient having antepartum care or will be having postpartum care with the obstetrician delivering the baby, eliminating multiple choice answers B and D.

In ICD-10-CM Alphabetic Index look for Delivery/cesarean/without indication referring you to O82; Outcome of delivery/single NEC/live born referring you to code Z37.0; and Pregnancy/weeks of gestation/39 weeks referring you to Z3A.39. Verify codes in the Tabular List.

117.   C. 57250

Patient is having a repair for a rectocele, not a cystocele, eliminating multiple choice answers B and D. Selection of the code is based surgical approach and whether performed anterior or posterior. The repair of rectocele was an open surgery performed by a "posterior" colporrhaphy approach, eliminating multiple choice answer A.

118.   C. 61343

The keywords in this craniectomy procedure to guide you to the correct code are: cervical (C-1 and C-2) laminectomy, medulla, and Chiari malformation found in the code description of 61343.

119.   D. 64490, 64491, 64492

The patient is having the injection in the paravertebral facet joints, eliminating multiple choice answers A and C. The selection of the injection(s) in the paravertebral facet joint codes are based on the region of the spine and

the number of levels injected. The code
description for code 64490 is for the thoracic
and has fluoroscopic guidance included in the
code, meaning code 77003 is not reported
separately. Also there is a parenthetical note
under code 64492 that indicates not to report
64492 more than once per day, eliminating
multiple choice answer B.

120.   B. 67924-E2

The procedure being performed is an entropion
repair on the left lower eyelid, eliminating
multiple choice answers A and D. This is an
extensive repair because a tarsal strip was
performed, eliminating multiple choice C.
HCPCS modifier E2 indicates that the procedure
is performed on the lower left eyelid.

121.   C. 99212

According to CPT® Evaluation and Management
(E/M) Service Guidelines subsection New and
Established Patient indicates: An established
patient is one who has received professional

face-to-face services from the physician/qualified health care professional or another physician/qualified health care professional of the exact same specialty and subspecialty who belongs to the same group practice, within the past three years. This eliminates multiple choices A and B. An established office visit requires at least 2 of 3 key components must meet or exceed the stated requirements to qualify for a particular level of E/M service. In the question you have: Problem Focused History + Expanded Problem Focused Exam + Straightforward MDM. The correct answer is 99212 because the two key components that meet are: Problem Focused History and Straightforward Medical Decision Making.

122.   C. 99203

Evaluation and Management Services Guidelines indicate for an office visit of a new patient all three key components (history, exam, and medical decision making) need to meet or exceed the stated requirements to qualify for that E/M service. In our question we have the following: Detailed History, Detailed Exam, and High complexity Medical Decision Making. The highest level that can be reached is 99203:

Detailed History - Meets

Detailed Examination - Meets

Medical Decision Making of Low Complexity - Exceeds

You can also determine the E/M level that requires all three key components another way. When all three key components do not exactly meet the E/M level, you report the E/M level that has the lowest key component(s) in the question. The correct code is 99203 because the lowest key components in the question are Detailed History and Detailed Exam.

123.   A. 99291-25, 36555, 31500

According to the CPT® subsection guidelines for Inpatient Neonatal and Pediatric Critical Care: To report critical care services provided in the outpatient setting (example, emergency department or office) for neonates and pediatric patients of any age, see the Critical Care codes 99291, 99292. This would eliminate multiple choice D. There is documentation in which the ER physician spent a total of 30 minutes on a critical patient, eliminating multiple choice C. Blood gas (82803) is a lab procedure that is not separately reported when billing for critical care. A list of services included in reporting critical care is found in the subsection guidelines under Critical Care Services. Modifier 25 is appended to 99291 to identify the evaluation and management service as a separately identifiable service in which billable procedures were performed on the same date of service.

124.   D. 99213, J02.0 H65.193

An established patient office visit codes requires 2 of the 3 key components (history, exam and medical decision making) to qualify for a particular level of E/M service. The documentation in the scenario provides: Expanded Problem Focused History, Expanded Problem Focused Exam, and Medical Decision Making of moderate complexity. The two key components that meet are Expanded Problem Focused History and Expanded Problem Focused Exam, selecting code 99213.

The strep culture for the pharyngitis came back positive for strep. Look in ICD-10-CM Alphabetic for Pharyngitis/streptococcal guiding you to code J02.0. Next look for Otitis/media/with effusion-see Otitis, media, non-suppurative. Look for Otitis/media/non-suppurative/acute or subacute guiding you to code H65.19-. Go to Tabular List to complete code, H65.193.

125. **A. 00400-QX-QS**

Look in the CPT® Index for Anesthesia/Integumentary System/Anterior Trunk referring you to 00400 which is the correct code. The HCPCS modifier QX is appended to report the service was provided by a medically directed CRNA. Modifier QS is appended to identify that the type of anesthesia is MAC or monitored anesthesia care.

126. **A. 00567, 6 hours**

The procedure performed is a coronary artery bypass. Look in the CPT® Index, for Anesthesia/Heart/Coronary Artery Bypass Grafting referring you to 00566 and 00567. The question indicates that the heart and lung bypass was used. Select 00567 because the code description includes "with pump oxygenator." Pump oxygenator describes when a cardiopulmonary bypass (CPB) machine is used to function as the heart and lungs during a heart or great vessel surgery.

The anesthesia start time is 6:00 PM and the anesthesia ends at 12:00 AM which is six hours.

Refer to the CPT® Anesthesia Guidelines under heading Time Reporting for reporting anesthesia time. Per the guidelines anesthesia time begins when the anesthesiologist begins to prepare the patient and ends when the anesthesiologist releases the patient under postoperative supervision. Surgical times are not reported for anesthesia time.

127.   C. 77078

This radiological service is a bone density study using computed tomography (CT) to asses bone mass or density of the spine. The correct code is 77078 to indicate that the study was completed with a CT or computed tomography on the spinal area.

128.   B. 76816, 76816-59

This is a follow-up ultrasound because she is being reassessed due to a previous ultrasound that showed abnormalities of the fetuses. The patient has twins and a parenthetical note under 76816 indicates to report 76816 with modifier 59 for each additional fetus.

129. B. 37197, T82.514A

Patient is having a broken tip of a catheter removed from the right ventricle, eliminating multiple choices A and D. Catheter was fractured eliminating choice C. The procedure includes imaging guidance so radiology code is not reported separately. The fracture of the port-a-cath is a mechanical complication. Look in the Alphabetic Index for Complication/catheter (device) NEC/intravenous infusion/mechanical/breakdown T82.514-. Go to the Tabular List to complete the code, T82.514A.

130. A. 49083

Patient is having an abdominal paracentesis performed, eliminating multiple choice answers B and D. The needle placement to withdraw the fluid was done under ultrasonic (imaging) guidance, eliminating multiple choice answer C. There is a parenthetical note under procedure code 49083 that states: Do not report 49083 in conjunction with 76942, 77002, 77012, and 77021.

131.   B. 88267, 88280, 88285

The chromosome analysis was taken from amniotic fluid eliminating multiple choices A, C and D. The selection of the codes are based on the type of sample used, the number of karyotypes performed, and the number of cells studied. There were two karyotypes performed with analyzing 30 cells. Code 88267 identifies the sample as amniotic fluid with only one karyotype and 15 cells studied. Code 88280 is reported for the additional karyotype. Code 88285 is reported for the remaining 15 cells.

132.   B. 89260, 89280

Sperm isolation is performed. Sperm washing refers to separating the sperm from semen and getting rid of dead or slow-moving sperm as well as additional chemicals that may impair fertilization (89260). The selection of the second listed code is for the number of oocytes fertilized. The correct code is 89280 to indicate less than 10 were fertilized.

133.   A. 88325

In the CPT® Index, look for Surgical Pathology/Consultation referring you to 88321-88325. 88325 is the correct code. The correct code is 88325 to indicate that the comprehensive consultation is being done by reviewing the patient's records and on specimens from a different facility. Code 99244 is reported when the consultation is involving the examination and evaluation of the patient. Code 88323 is the consultation and report on referred material requiring preparing of slides. Code 88329 is when a consultation is performed during a surgery.

134.   D. 97535 x 3, I69.959

The selection of the code is based on the type of activities completed in the session, the use of equipment used in the training, and the amount of time the session lasted. The therapist is at the patient's home site to teach home management for self-care, guiding you to code 97535 reporting the code three times to indicate the total time of 45 minutes were spent with the patient.

The patient has a residual effect of hemiparesis from having a CVA. According to ICD-10-CM Coding Guidelines, I.C.9.d.1, Category I69 is used to indicate conditions classifiable to categories I60-I67 as the causes of sequela (neurologic deficits), themselves classified elsewhere. These "late effects" include neurologic deficits that persist after initial onset of conditions classifiable to I60-I67. The late effect codes for CVA's are combination codes which means code I69.959 reports both the residual and cause in one code. In the ICD-10-CM Alphabetic Index look for Hemiparesis which directs you to see Hemiplegia. Look for Hemiplegia/following cerebrovascular disease referring you to I69.959.

135.   B. 92603

The coding scenario deals with a cochlear
implant, eliminating multiple choice D. The
patient is 10 years-old with a cochlear implant,
eliminating multiple choice A. The selection of
the remaining codes is based on the age of the
patient and the current encounter as new vs
subsequent. There is no documentation relating
to a previous attempt to program the implant.
The placement of the cochlear implant was
recent, so this is not a subsequent
reprogramming, eliminating multiple choice C.

136.   C. 93303-26

Selection of the codes are based on the
technique used. Infant is having the
echocardiogram performed through the chest
(transthoracic) not through the device in the
esophagus (transesophageal), eliminating
multiple choices B and D. Given the age of the
patient, the use of the congenital code is
correct. Congenital referring to a deformity at
birth. The subsection guidelines for
Echocardiography in the CPT® codebook states:

When interpretation is performed separately, use modifier 26. Modifier 26 needs to be appended because only the interpretation of the echocardiogram was performed by the pediatrician.

137.   C. Urinary

Glomerulonephritis is a form of nephritis marked by inflammation of the glomeruli of the kidney. In the ICD-10-CM Alphabetic Index look for Glomerulonephritis referring you to code N05.9. In the Tabular List this code is found Chapter 14: Diseases of Genitourinary System.

138.   A. Upper end of the arm

The humerus is the bone extending from the shoulder to the elbow. Most resources define proximal to the area nearest to the trunk of the body. In the ICD-10-CM Alphabetic Index, look for Fracture, traumatic/humerus/proximal end refers you to see Fracture, humerus, upper end.

139.   B. Manipulation

In the CPT® codebook in the section for Musculoskeletal System guidelines defines Manipulation: is used throughout the musculoskeletal fracture and dislocation subsections to specifically mean the attempted reduction or restoration of a fracture or joint dislocation to its normal anatomic alignment by the application of manually applied force.

140.   B. Deficiency of sperm in semen

The breakdown of this term: combining form olig/o means too few or too little and spermia refers to the condition of the sperm. The definition is too low or too few sperm. In the Alphabetic Index look for Oligospermia N64.11. In the Tabular List oligospermia is indicated as a type of male infertility.

141.   B. Chest cavity

The breakdown of this term: thorac/o refers to chest or thorax and the suffix -centesis refers to puncture; the insertion of a needle or similar instrument into a bodily space to add or withdraw fluids. In the CPT® Index look for Thoracentesis referring you to codes 32554, 32555. There is a diagram in the CPT® codebook for these codes that indicate the procedures are for removal of accumulated fluid or air from the pleural space between the ribs.

142.   C. Blood Vessels

The breakdown of this term is: Angi/o refers to blood vessel and the suffix -gram refers to a written record. An angiogram is an X-ray photograph or an imaging technique that uses contrast/dye to look inside blood vessels. Look in CPT® Index for Angiography referring you to codes in the Radiology section in which many arteries are listed in alphabetical order.

143.   B. Ball-and-socket joint, hinge joint, and saddle point

There are six types of freely moving or synovial joints: ball-and-socket, hinge, pivot, condyloid, saddle, and gliding joints.

144.   B. G97.61

ICD-10-CM guidelines (Section IV.H) indicate uncertain diagnosis that is documented as probable, suspected, rule out, or etc. are not coded. This eliminates multiple choice answers A and D. The patient is in a post-operative period because she is going back to the OR when just having a laminectomy performed and there was found a hematoma. This eliminates multiple choice C. This is a complication of the procedure, because a hematoma was found. Look in the Alphabetic Index for Complication/postprocedural/hematoma/nervous system/following a nervous system procedure referring you to code G97.61.

145.   A. I11.0, I50.9

In the ICD-10-CM Alphabetic Index look for Hypertension/due to/heart disease/with/heart failure (congestive) referring you to code I11.0. This eliminates multiple choice answers B and C. In the Tabular List under code I11.0 there is an instructional note to Use additional code to identify type of heart failure (I50.-). Code I50.9 (Congestive heart failure) is reported as the second code.

146. A. Q4012

The selection of the code is based on the materials used, the length of the cast, and the age of the patient. The patient being 10 years-old getting a short arm fiberglass cast guides you to select code Q4012.

147. B. J7306

When reviewing each code in the HCPCS Level II codebook, code J7306 is the correct code to report for the Levonorgestrel implant and supplies.

148. D. Reasonable and necessary conditions of coverage for an item or service Local Coverage Determinations (LCD) are Medicare Administrative Contractor rules indicating whether or not a particular item or service is

covered. Most LCDs also provide a list of diagnosis codes for which a procedure may be covered; however, because other issues factor into payment, coverage is not guaranteed. Modifier guidelines and fee schedule information is included in the annual Medicare Physician Fee Schedule. National Correct Coding Initiative (NCCI) is used to know what CPT® codes are bundled.

149.   C. 24

Place of service codes are two digit numerical codes that define the location where services are performed and reported on the CMS-1500 form. A complete chart of Place-Of-Service codes is found on the first page in CPT® codebook. A service provided in an ASC is reported with POS code 24.

150.   C. As STEMI

ICD-10-CM guidelines (Section I.C.9.e.1) indicate: If STEMI converts to NSTEMI due to thrombolytic therapy, it is still coded as STEMI.

Made in the USA
Coppell, TX
11 May 2021

55426073R00142